From th

Welcome to our extra-special new astrological forecast which takes you ɑ up to the end of the century on Decei our year-ahead guides all the astrologi ... be made using tables and a calculator. Today, by the miracle of computers, we have been able to build our knowledge and hard work into a program which calculates the precise astrological aspect for every day in a flash.

When Shakespeare wrote 'The fault, dear Brutus, is not in our stars, but in ourselves', he spoke for every astrologer. In our day-to-day forecasts we cannot hope to be 100% accurate every time, because this would remove the most important influence in your life, which is you! What we can hope to do is to give you a sense of the astrological backdrop to the day, week or month in question, and so prompt you to think a little harder about what is going in your own life, and thus help improve your chances of acting effectively to deal with events and situations.

During the course of a year, there may be one or two readings that are similar in nature. This is not an error, it is simply that the Moon or a planet has repeated a particular pattern. In addition, a planetary pattern that applies to your sign may apply to someone else's sign at some other point during the year. One planetary 'return' that you already know well is the Solar return that occurs every year on your birthday.

If you've read our guides before, you'll know that we're never less than positive and that our advice is unpretentious, down to earth, and rooted in daily experience. If this is the first time you've met us, please regard us not as in any way astrological gurus, but as good friends who wish you nothing but health, prosperity and contentment. Happy 1998-9!

Sasha Fenton is a world-renowned astrologer, palmist and Tarot card reader, with over 80 books published on Astrology, Palmistry, Tarot and other forms of divination. Now living in London, Sasha is a regular broadcaster on radio and television, as well as making frequent contributions to newspapers and magazines around the world, including South Africa and Australia. She is a former President and Secretary of the British Astrological and Psychic Society (BAPS) and Secretary of the Advisory Panel on Astrological Education.

Jonathan Dee is an astrologer, artist and historian based in Wales, and a direct descendant of the great Elizabethan alchemist and wizard Dr John Dee, court astrologer to Queen Elizabeth I. He has written a number of books, including the recently completed *The Chronicles of Ancient Egypt,* and for the last five years has co-written an annual astrological forecast series with Sasha Fenton. A regular broadcaster on television and radio, he has also hosted the Starline show for KQED Talk Radio, New Mexico.

YOUR DAY-BY-DAY FORECAST
SEPTEMBER 1998 – DECEMBER 1999

SASHA FENTON • JONATHAN DEE

HALDANE • MASON

Zambezi

DEDICATION
For the memory of Gary Bailey, a new star in heaven.

ACKNOWLEDGEMENTS
With many thanks to our computer wizard, Sean Lovatt.

This edition published 1998
by Haldane Mason Ltd
59 Chepstow Road
London W2 5BP

Copyright © Sasha Fenton and Jonathan Dee 1998

All rights reserved. No part of this publication may be reproduced, stored in a retrieval system, or transmitted, in any form or by any means, electronic, mechanical, photocopying, recording or otherwise, without the prior permission of the publishers.

Sasha Fenton and Jonathan Dee assert the moral right to be identified as the authors of this work.

ISBN 1-902463-05-6

Designed and produced by Haldane Mason Ltd
Cover illustration by Lo Cole
Edited by Jan Budkowski

Printed in Singapore by Craft Print Pte Ltd

CONTENTS

AN ASTROLOGICAL OVERVIEW OF THE 20TH CENTURY	6
THE ESSENTIAL CAPRICORN	16
YOUR SUN SIGN	19
ALL THE OTHER SUN SIGNS	21
YOU AND YOURS	29
YOUR RISING SIGN	36
CAPRICORN IN LOVE	41
YOUR PROSPECTS FOR 1999	43
CAPRICORN IN THE FINAL QUARTER OF 1998	46
CAPRICORN IN 1999	70

An Astrological Overview of the 20th Century

Next year the shops will be full of astrology books for the new century and also for the new millennium. In this book, the last of the old century, we take a brief look back to see where the slow-moving outer planets were in each decade and what it meant. Obviously this will be no more than a very brief glance backwards but next year you will be able to see the picture in much more depth when we bring out our own book for the new millennium.

1900 - 1909

The century began with Pluto in Gemini and it was still in Gemini by the end of the decade. Neptune started out in Gemini but moved into cancer in 1901 and ended the decade still in Cancer. Uranus started the century in Sagittarius, moving to Capricorn in 1904 and ending the decade still in Capricorn. Saturn began the century in Sagittarius, moving to Capricorn in January 1900 and then through Aquarius, Pisces and Aries, ending the decade in Aries.

The stars and the decade

In general terms, the planet of upheaval in the dynastic sign of Sagittarius with Saturn also in that sign and Pluto opposing it, all at the very start of the century put the spotlight on dynasties, royalty and empires. As Saturn left for the 'establishment' sign of Capricorn these just about held together but as the decade ended, the power and control that these ancient dynasties had were loosening their grip on the developed world of the time. Queen Victoria died in 1901 and her son, Edward VII was dying by the end of the decade, so in Britain, the Victorian age of certainty was already coming to an end. The Boer War was only just won by Britain in 1902 which brought a shock to this successful colonial country.

Pluto in Gemini brought a transformation in methods of communications. It was as Saturn entered the innovative sign of Aquarius that these took concrete and useful form. Thus it was during this decade that the motor car, telephone, typewriter, gramophone and colour photography came into existence. Air travel began in 1900 with the first Zeppelin airship flight, the first powered aeroplane flight by the Wright brothers in 1904 and Louis Blériot's flight across the English Channel in 1909. Edison demonstrated the Kinetophone, the first machine capable of showing talking moving pictures in

1910. Even the nature of war changed as technologically modern Japan managed to fight off the might of the Russian empire in the war of 1904 - 1905.

The Treaty of Versailles, followed by further treaties of Aix and Trianon served to crush the German nation and therefore sow the seeds of the next war.

1910 – 1919

Pluto opened the decade in Gemini, moving to Cancer in 1913. Neptune travelled from Cancer to Leo in September 1914 while Uranus moved out of Capricorn, through Aquarius to end the decade in Pisces. Saturn moved from Aries to Taurus, then to Gemini, back into Taurus, then into Gemini again entering Cancer in 1914, then on through Leo and ending the decade in Virgo.

The stars and the decade

Now we see the start of a pattern. Sagittarius may be associated with dynasties but it is the home-loving and patriotic signs of Cancer and Leo that actually seem to be associated with major wars. The desire either to expand a country's domestic horizons or to protect them from the expansion of others is ruled by the maternal sign of Cancer, followed by the paternal one of Leo. Home, family, tradition, safety all seem to be fought over when major planets move through these signs. When future generations learn about the major wars of the 20th century they will probably be lumped together in their minds - despite the 20-year gap between them - just as we lump the Napoleonic wars together, forgetting that there was a nine-year gap between them, and of course, this long stay of Pluto in Cancer covered the whole of this period.

It is interesting to note that Pluto moved into Cancer in July 1913 and Neptune entered Leo on the 23rd of September 1914, just three of weeks after the outbreak of the First World War. Saturn moved into Cancer in April 1914. Pluto is associated with transformation, Neptune with dissolution and Saturn with loss, sadness and sickness. Many people suffered and so many families and dynasties were unexpectedly dissolved at that time, among these, the Romanov Czar and his family and the kings of Portugal, Hungary, Italy and Germany and the Manchu dynasty of China. America (born on the 4th of July, 1776 and therefore a Cancerian country) was thrust into prominence as a major economic and social power after this war. Russia experienced the Bolshevik revolution during it. As Saturn moved into Virgo (the sign that is associated with health) at the end of this decade, a world-wide plague of influenza killed 20 million people, far more than had died during the course of the war itself.

CAPRICORN

1920 - 1929

The roaring 20s began and ended with Pluto in Cancer. Neptune moved from Leo to Virgo at the end of this decade and Uranus moved from Pisces to Aries in 1927. Saturn travelled from Virgo, through Libra, Scorpio, Sagittarius and then backwards and forwards between Sagittarius and Capricorn, ending up in Capricorn at the end of 1929.

The stars and the decade

Pluto's long transformative reign in Cancer made life hard for men during this time. Cancer is the most female of all the signs, being associated with nurturing and motherhood. Many men were sick in mind and body as a result of the war and women began to take proper jobs for the first time. Family planning and better living conditions brought improvements in life for ordinary people and in the developed world there was a major boom in house building as well as in improved road and rail commuter systems. The time of lords and ladies was passing and ordinary people were demanding better conditions. Strikes and unrest were common, especially in Germany. As the decade ended, the situation both domestically and in the foreign policies of the developed countries began to look up. Even the underdeveloped countries began to modernize a little. Shortly before the middle of this decade, all the politicians who might have prevented the rise of Hitler and the Nazi party died and then came the stock market crash of 1929. The probable astrological sequence that set this train of circumstances off was the run up to the opposition of Saturn in Capricorn to Pluto in Cancer which took place in 1931. The effects of such major planetary events are often felt while the planets are closing into a conjunction or opposition etc., rather than just at the time of their exactitude.

On a brighter note great strides were made in the worlds of art, music and film and ordinary people could enjoy more entertainment than ever before, in 1929 the first colour television was demonstrated and in 1928 Alexander Fleming announced his discovery of penicillin. At the very start of the decade prohibition passed into US Federal law, ushering in the age of organized crime and as a spin-off a great increase in drinking in that country and later on, all those wonderful gangster films. The same year, the partition of Ireland took place bringing more conflict and this time on a very long-term basis.

1930 - 1939

The 1930s should have been better than the 1920s but they were not. Pluto remained in Cancer until 1937, Neptune remained in Virgo throughout the decade, Uranus entered Taurus in 1934 and Saturn moved from Capricorn through Aquarius, Pisces then back and forth between Aries and Pisces, ending the decade in Taurus.

The stars and the decade

Neptune's voyage through Virgo did help in the field of advances in medicine and in public health. Pluto continued to make life hard for men and then by extension for families, while in the 'motherhood' sign of Cancer. While Saturn was in the governmental signs of Capricorn and Aquarius, democracy ceased to exist anywhere in the world. In the UK a coalition government was in power for most of the decade while in the USA, Franklin Delano Roosevelt ruled as a kind of benign emperor for almost three terms of office, temporarily dismantling much of that country's democratic machinery while he did so. Governments in Russia, Germany, Italy, Spain and Japan moved to dictatorships or dictatorial types of government with all the resultant tyranny, while France, Britain and even the USA floundered for much of the time. China was ruled by warring factions. However, there was an upsurge of popular entertainment at this time, especially through the mediums of film, music and radio probably due to the advent of adventurous, inventive Uranus into the music and entertainment sign of Taurus in 1934.

1940 - 1949

War years once again. Pluto remained in the 'paternal' sign of Leo throughout this decade, bringing tyranny and control of the masses in all the developed countries and also much of the Third World. Neptune entered Libra in 1942, Uranus moved from Taurus to Gemini in 1941, then to Cancer in 1948. Saturn began the decade in Taurus, moved to Gemini, Cancer, Leo and finally Virgo during this decade. The 'home and country' signs of Cancer and Leo were once more thrust into the limelight in a war context. Neptune is not a particularly warlike planet and Libra is normally a peaceable sign but Libra does rule open enemies as well as peace and harmony.

The stars and the decade

To continue looking for the moment at the planet Neptune, astrologers don't take its dangerous side seriously enough. Neptune can use the sea in a particularly destructive manner when it wants to with tidal waves, disasters at sea and so on, so it is interesting to note that the war in the West was almost lost for the allies at sea due to the success of the German U-boats. Hitler gambled on a quick end to the war in the east and shut his mind to Napoleon's experience of the Russian winter. Saturn through Cancer and Leo, followed by the inventive sign of Uranus entering Cancer at the end of the decade almost brought home, family, tradition and the world itself to an end with the explosions of the first atomic bombs.

However, towards the end of this decade, it became clear that democracy, the rights of ordinary people and a better lifestyle for everybody were a better answer than trying to find 'lebensraum' by pinching one's neighbour's land and enslaving its population. Saturn's entry into Virgo brought great advances in medicine and the plagues and diseases of the past began to diminish throughout the world. Pluto in Leo transformed the power structures of every country and brought such ideas as universal education, better housing and social security systems - at least in the developed world.

1950 - 1959

Pluto still dipped in and out of Leo until it finally left for Virgo in 1957. Neptune finally left Libra for Scorpio in 1955, Uranus sat on that dangerous and warlike cusp of Cancer and Leo, while Saturn moved swiftly through Virgo, Libra, Scorpio, Sagittarius and then into Capricorn.

The stars and the decade

The confrontations between dictators and between dictatorships and democracy continued during this time with the emphasis shifting to the conflict between communism and capitalism. The Korean war started the decade and the communist take-over in China ended it. Military alertness was reflected in the UK by the two years of national service that young men were obliged to perform throughout the decade. Rationing, shortages of food, fuel and consumer goods remained in place for half the decade, but by the end of it, the world was becoming a very different place. With American money, Germany and Japan were slowly rebuilt, communism did at least bring a measure of stability in China and the Soviet Union, although its pervasive power brought fear and peculiar witch hunts in the United States. In Europe and the USA the lives of ordinary people improved beyond belief.

Pluto in Virgo brought plenty of work for the masses and for ordinary people, poverty began to recede for the first time in history. Better homes, labour-saving devices and the vast amount of popular entertainment in the cinema, the arts, popular music and television at long last brought fun into the lives of most ordinary folk. In Britain and the Commonwealth, in June 1953, the coronation of the new Queen ushered in a far more optimistic age while her Empire dissolved around her.

CAPRICORN

1960 - 1969

This is the decade that today's middle-aged folk look back on with fond memories, yet it was not always as safe as we like to think. Pluto remained in Virgo throughout the decade bringing work and better health to many people. Neptune remained in Scorpio throughout this time, while Uranus traversed back and forth between Leo and Virgo, then from Virgo to Libra, ending the decade in Libra. Saturn hovered around the cusp of Taurus and Gemini until the middle of the decade and then on through Gemini and Cancer, spending time around the Cancer/Leo cusp and then on through Leo to rest once again on the Leo/Virgo cusp.

The stars and the decade

The Cancer/Leo threats of atomic war were very real in the early 1960s, with the Cuban missile crisis bringing America and the Soviet Union to the point of war. The Berlin wall went up. President Kennedy's assassination in November 1963 shocked the world and the atmosphere of secrets, spies and mistrust abounded in Europe, the USA and in the Soviet Union. One of the better manifestations of this time of cold war, CIA dirty tricks and spies was the plethora of wonderful spy films and television programmes of the early 60s. Another was the sheer fun of the Profumo affair!

The late 1960s brought the start of a very different atmosphere. The Vietnam War began to be challenged by the teenagers whose job it was to die in it and the might of America was severely challenged by these tiny Vietcong soldiers in black pyjamas and sandals. The wave of materialism of the 1950s was less attractive to the flower-power generation of the late 60s. The revolutionary planet Uranus in balanced Libra brought the protest movement into being and an eventual end to racial segregation in the USA. Equality between the sexes was beginning to be considered. The troubles of Northern Ireland began at the end of this decade.

In 1969, Neil Armstrong stepped out onto the surface of the Moon, thereby marking the start of a very different age, the New Age, the Age of Aquarius.

1970 - 1979

Pluto began the decade around the Virgo/Libra cusp, settling in Libra in 1972 and remaining there for the rest of the decade. Neptune started the decade by moving back and forth between Scorpio and Sagittarius and residing in Sagittarius for the rest of the decade. Uranus hovered between Libra and Scorpio until 1975 and then travelled through Scorpio until the end of the decade while Saturn moved from Taurus to Gemini, then hung around the Cancer/Leo cusp and finally moved into Virgo.

CAPRICORN

The stars and the decade

The planets in or around that dangerous Cancer/Leo cusp and the continuing Libran emphasis brought more danger from total war as America struggled with Vietnam and the cold war. However, the influence of Virgo brought work, an easier life and more hope than ever to ordinary people in the First World. Uranus in Libra brought different kinds of love partnerships into public eye as fewer people bothered to marry. Divorce became easier and homosexuality became legal. With Uranus opening the doors to secretive Scorpio, spies such as Burgess, Maclean, Philby, Lonsdale and Penkowski began to come in from the cold. President Nixon was nicely caught out at Watergate, ushering in a time of more openness in governments everywhere.

If you are reading this book, you may be doing so because you are keen to know about yourself and your sign, but you are likely to be quite interested in astrology and perhaps in other esoteric techniques. You can thank the atmosphere of the 1970s for the openness and the lack of fear and superstition which these subjects now enjoy. The first festival of Mind, Body and Spirit took place in 1976 and the British Astrological and Psychic Society was launched in the same year, both of these events being part of the increasing interest in personal awareness and alternative lifestyles.

Neptune in Scorpio brought fuel crises and Saturn through Cancer and Leo brought much of the repression of women to an end, with some emancipation from tax and social anomalies. Tea bags and instant coffee allowed men for the first time to cope with the terrible hardship of making a cuppa!

1980 - 1989

Late in 1983, Pluto popped into the sign of Scorpio, popped out again and re-entered it in 1984. Astrologers of the 60s and 70s feared this planetary situation in case it brought the ultimate Plutonic destruction with it. Instead of this, the Soviet Union and South Africa freed themselves from tyranny and the Berlin Wall came down. The main legacy of Pluto in Scorpio is the Scorpionic association of danger through sex, hence the rise of AIDS. Neptune began the decade in Sagittarius then it travelled back and forth over the Sagittarius/Capricorn cusp, ending the decade in Capricorn. Uranus moved from Scorpio, back and forth over the Scorpio/Sagittarius cusp, then through Sagittarius, ending the decade in Capricorn. Saturn began the decade in Virgo, then hovered around the Virgo/Libra cusp, through Libra, Scorpio and Sagittarius, resting along the Sagittarius/Capricorn cusp, ending the decade in Capricorn.

CAPRICORN

The stars and the decade
The movement of planets through the dynastic sign of Sagittarius brought doubt and uncertainty to Britain's royal family, while the planets in authoritative Capricorn brought strong government to the UK in the form of Margaret Thatcher. Ordinary people began to seriously question the *status quo* and to attempt to change it. Even in the hidden empire of China, modernization and change began to creep in. Britain went to war again by sending the gunboats to the Falkland Islands to fight off a truly old-fashioned takeover bid by the daft Argentinean dictator, General Galtieri.

Saturn is an earth planet, Neptune rules the sea, while Uranus is associated with the air. None of these planets was in their own element and this may have had something to do with the increasing number of natural and man-made disasters that disrupted the surface of the earth during this decade. The first space shuttle flight took place in 1981 and the remainder of the decade reflected many people's interest in extra-terrestrial life in the form of films and television programmes. ET went home. Black rap music and the casual use of drugs became a normal part of the youth scene. Maybe the movement of escapist Neptune through the 'outer space' sign of Sagittarius had something to do with this.

1990 - 1999
Pluto began the decade in Scorpio, moving in and out of Sagittarius until 1995 remaining there for the rest of the decade. Neptune began the decade in Capricorn, travelling back and forth over the cusp of Aquarius, ending the decade in Aquarius, Uranus moved in and out of Aquarius, remaining there from 1996 onwards. Saturn travelled from Capricorn, through Aquarius, Pisces (and back again), then on through Pisces, Aries, in and out of Taurus, finally ending the decade in Taurus.

The stars and the decade
The Aquarian emphasis has brought advances in science and technology and a time when computers are common even in the depths of darkest Africa. The logic and fairness of Aquarius does seem to have affected many of the peoples of the earth. Pluto in the open sign of Sagittarius brought much governmental secrecy to an end, it will also transform the traditional dynasties of many countries before it leaves them for good. The aftermath of the dreadful and tragic death of Princess Diana in 1997 put a rocket under the creaking 19th-century habits of British royalty.

The final decade began with yet another war – this time the Gulf War – which sent a serious signal to all those who fancy trying their hand at international bullying or the 19th-century tactics of pinching your neighbour's land and resources. Uranus's last fling in Capricorn tore up the earth with volcanoes and earthquakes, and its stay in Aquarius seems to be keeping this pattern going. Saturn in Pisces, opposite the 'health' sign of Virgo is happily bringing new killer viruses into being and encouraging old ones to build up resistance to antibiotics. The bubonic plague is alive and well in tropical countries along with plenty of other plagues that either are, or are becoming resistant to modern medicines. Oddly enough the planetary line-up in 1997 was similar to that of the time of the great plague of London in 1665!

Films, the arts, architecture all showed signs of beginning an exciting period of revolution in 1998. Life became more electronic and computer-based for the younger generation while in the old world, the vast army of the elderly began to struggle with a far less certain world of old-age poverty and strange and frightening innovations. Keeping up to date and learning to adapt is the only way to survive now, even for the old folks.

It is interesting to note that the first event of importance to shock Europe in this century was the morganatic marriage of Franz Ferdinand, the heir to the massively powerful Austro-Hungarian throne. This took place in the summer of 1900. The unpopularity of this controlling and repressive empire fell on its head in Sarajevo on the 28th of July 1914. This mighty empire is now almost forgotten, but its death throes are still being played out in and around Sarajevo today - which only goes to show how long it can take for anything to be settled.

Technically the twentieth century only ends at the beginning of the year 2001 but most of us will be celebrating the end of the century and the end of the millennium and the end of the last day of 1999 - that is if we are all here of course! A famous prediction of global disaster comes from the writings of the French writer, doctor and astrologer Nostradamus (1503–66):

- The year 1999, seventh month,
- From the sky will come a great King of Terror:
- To bring back to life the great King of the Mongols,
- Before and after Mars reigns.
  (Quatrain X:72 from the *Centuries*)

Jonathan has worked out that with the adjustments of the calendar from the time of Nostradamus, the date of the predicted disaster will be the 11th of August 1999. As it happens there will be a total eclipse of the Sun at ten past eleven on that day at 18 degrees of Leo. We have already seen how the signs of Cancer, Leo and Libra seem to be the ones that are most clearly associated with war and this reference to 'Mars reigning' is the fact that Mars is the god of war. Therefore, the prediction suggests that an Oriental king will wage a war from the sky that brings terror to the world. Some people have suggested that this event would bring about the end of the world but that is not what the prediction actually says. A look back over the 1900s has proved this whole century to be one of terror from the skies but it would be awful to think that there would be yet another war, this time emanating from Mongolia. Terrible but not altogether impossible to imagine I guess. Well, let us hope that we are all here for us to write and for you to enjoy the next set of zodiac books for the turn of the millennium and beyond.

2000 onwards: a very brief look forward

The scientific exploration and eventual colonization of space is on the way now. Scorpio rules fossil fuels and there will be no major planets passing through this sign for quite a while so alternative fuel sources will have to be sought. Maybe it will be the entry of Uranus into the pioneering sign of Aries in January 2012 that will make a start on this. The unusual line up of the 'ancient seven' planets of Sun, Moon, Mercury, Venus, Mars and Saturn in Taurus on the 5th of May 2000 will be interesting. Taurus represents such matters as land, farming, building, cooking, flowers, the sensual beauty of music, dancing and the arts. Jonathan and Sasha will work out the astrological possibilities for the future in depth and put out ideas together for you in a future book.

CAPRICORN

The Essential Capricorn

YOUR RULING PLANET Your ruling body is Saturn. This rather gloomy Roman god represents limitations and hard lessons in life but the musical and cheerful god, Pan, is also associated with Capricorn.

YOUR SYMBOL The goat is your symbol. Capricorn is said to represent the mythical goat Amalthea, who suckled Jupiter in his infancy. Playfully, the baby god pulled off one of his horns which then became the cornucopia, or horn of plenty. The merry, goat-footed god, Pan, is also associated with your sign. In a sure-footed Capricorn manner, the mountain goat climbs onwards and upwards.

PARTS OF THE BODY The skin, ears, bones, knees and teeth. Capricorn is also associated with chronic ailments.

YOUR GOOD BITS You work hard, look after your family and you have a sense of duty. You also have a nice, dry sense of humour. You are realistic.

YOUR BAD BITS You can be dull and dry, stingy and lacking in imagination.

YOUR WEAKNESSES Status symbols.

YOUR BEST DAY Saturday. This is the day associated with the Roman god, Saturn. Literally, Saturn's day.

YOUR WORST DAY Thursday. Probably because it is associated with the god Jupiter (Jove) who is opposite in nature to Saturn.

YOUR COLOURS Black, grey, dark green, brown.

CITIES Brussels, Delhi, Rio de Janeiro.

COUNTRIES The Balkans, the West Indies, Mexico, Lithuania, India, Mexico, Afghanistan.

HOLIDAYS You are fond of travelling and any opportunity to take fairly

CAPRICORN

gentle exercise, so a holiday by the sea with some sailing or walking might suit you.

YOUR FAVOURITE CAR You would probably enjoy owning some kind of all-weather, all-terrain vehicle, such as a jeep or a British Land-Rover. You probably complain about the cost of fuel!

YOUR FAVOURITE MEAL OUT You enjoy good food, well-cooked and presented and at a reasonable price. You may enjoy curries and spicy foods, and you are usually happy to eat what is put in front of you.

YOUR FAVOURITE DRINK You probably don't like wasting money on alcohol, but when you do drink you may prefer a small glass of brandy or a liqueur.

YOUR HERBS Sage, sorrel.

YOUR TREE Yew.

YOUR FLOWERS Pansy, hemlock, ivy, thistle.

YOUR ANIMALS Goat, donkey, elephant, toad.

YOUR METAL Lead.

YOUR GEMS There are a number of gems associated with your sign, including the turquoise, black opal and tourmaline.

MODE OF DRESS When young you prefer fairly formal clothes which are good quality and made to last. When you get older, you become a bit more adventurous with colours and styles.

YOUR CAREERS Dentist, doctor, lawyer, accountant, property dealer, financier, banker.

YOUR FRIENDS You respect people who are loyal, hard-working and fair but you are closest to your family, and friends come a long way behind them.

YOUR ENEMIES Feckless or stupid people who ignore authority.

CAPRICORN

YOUR FAVOURITE GIFT You may find it hard to indulge yourself, so anything that is utterly luxurious would suit you. A smart briefcase or desk set might suit males, with nice clothes or a trip to the beauticians for women. A night out with dinner and dancing on the menu would be good too. You appreciate a nice clock or watch, monogrammed stationery, CDs, a pair of climbing boots or an electronic diary.

YOUR IDEAL HOME If possible, you would choose to live in a warm country, or otherwise a home with excellent central heating! You can live in a flat, but you need to get out regularly to indulge in your hobbies and interests. You prefer to have your family fairly close by so they can visit you often.

YOUR FAVOURITE BOOKS Practical and 'how-to' books usually appeal, and anything that tells you how to make or invest money. Otherwise, you probably enjoy stimulating novels that spark discussions with your partner.

YOUR FAVOURITE MUSIC You may like the blues, classical music or music that you can dance to.

YOUR GAMES AND SPORTS Many Capricorns love to dance and you may also enjoy climbing, but team games are not really your thing. Board games that have a mathematical, financial or strategic element to them may please you – Monopoly, for example.

YOUR PAST AND FUTURE LIVES There are many theories about past lives and even some about future ones, but we suggest that your immediate past life was ruled by the sign previous to Capricorn and that your future life will be governed by the sign that follows Capricorn. Therefore you were Sagittarius in your previous life and will be Aquarius in the next. If you want to know all about either of these signs, zip straight out to the shops and buy our books on them!

YOUR LUCKY NUMBER Your lucky number is 1. To find your lucky number on a raffle ticket or something similar, first add the numbers together. For example, if one of your lottery numbers is 28, add 2 + 8 to make 10; then add 1 + 0, to give the root number of 1. The number 316 on a raffle ticket works in the same way. Add 3 + 1 + 6 to make 10: then add 1 + 0, making 1. As your lucky number is 1, such numbers as 1, 10, 100, 1000, 91, 181 or 271 would work well for you. A selection of lottery numbers should include some of the following: 1, 10, 19, 28, 37 and 46.

CAPRICORN

Your Sun Sign

Your Sun Sign is determined by your date of birth.
Thus anyone born between 21st March and 20th April is Aries and so
on through the calendar. Your Rising Sign (see page 36)
is determined by the day and time of your birth.

CAPRICORN

RULED BY SATURN
22nd December to 20th January

Yours is a feminine, earth sign whose symbol is the goat. This combination makes for a mixture of gentle passivity and determined assertion.

Astrology books tell us that Capricorns are ambitious, hard-working, materialistic and rather miserable people who have hard lives. Well, you certainly do work hard and are usually ambitious for yourself and your family. However, you aren't miserable or depressed and your life is no harder in total than anyone else's. I stress in total, because what actually happens is that trouble strikes you early on and you may have a difficult or deprived childhood or some unhappy early years. After the age of thirty, things pick up, getting even better after forty, leading to a happy and successful old age. You are shy and retiring and you don't push yourself forward. You are embarrassed if anyone puts you on show in any way. You make an excellent back-room boy or girl, working hard on various projects without making a fuss. However, you can complain terribly when you feel ill. You can be tough in business but you are rarely unreasonable. Like all earth-sign people, you work at your own speed and you hate to be rushed or hassled. You may be personally ambitious, but you also want your family to do well, and you will always spend money on education and holidays for them.

Some Capricorns are painfully shy and retiring while others are surprisingly outgoing. Even the shy ones become more confident and outgoing in middle age. You are clever, but you use your intelligence in a practical way rather than in an inventive or overly intellectual manner. Your brightness, coupled with your capacity for hard work and concentration, can bring you success in any number of fields. You have excellent public relations skills and a great deal of quiet charm. Your outer manner is slightly formal but pleasantly welcoming, and this makes you popular with working colleagues and friends alike. Your dry and gentle sense of humour and your sensitivity to the feelings of others endears you to people. However, very few people really know you at all well.

It is an unusual Capricorn who doesn't have a job. You enjoy being productive and you like to end each day feeling that you have done something useful with it. Some of you are personally ambitious and you will try to get as far up the career ladder as you can. Astrology books usually suggest that you do well in accountancy or banking and, while this is true for many of you, there are plenty of Capricorns in the media and the glamorous end of show business. Jon and Sasha have come across plenty of you in the worlds of publishing and broadcasting. Whatever you choose to do, you take a responsible and reliable attitude to it.

You also take a responsible attitude to your personal relationships and to family life, and you would do a good job of looking after stepchildren or in-laws if you had to. Many Capricorns are good-looking and enjoy a bit of harmless flirting. You are not promiscuous and you take your relationships seriously, trying to make even the most difficult ones work. You definitely prefer family relationships to friendship and you can usually be found in or around your home when you are not working. Some of you can sacrifice your family life for work, but most of you value it far too much to do that.

CAPRICORN

All the Other Sun Signs

ARIES
21st March to 20th April

Ariens can get anything they want off the ground, but they may land back down again with a bump. Quick to think and to act, Ariens are often intelligent and have little patience with fools. This includes anyone who is slower than themselves.

They are not the tidiest of people and they are impatient with details, except when engaged upon their special subject; then Ariens can fiddle around for hours. They are willing to make huge financial sacrifices for their families and they can put up with relatives living with them as long as this leaves them free to do their own thing. Aries women are decisive and competitive at work but many are disinterested in homemaking. They might consider giving up a relationship if it interfered with their ambitions. Highly sexed and experimental, they are faithful while in love but, if love begins to fade, they start to look around. Ariens may tell themselves that they are only looking for amusement, but they may end up in a fulfilling relationship with someone else's partner. This kind of situation offers the continuity and emotional support which they need with no danger of boredom or entrapment.

Their faults are those of impatience and impetuosity, coupled with a hot temper. They can pick a furious row with a supposed adversary, tear him or her to pieces then walk away from the situation five minutes later, forgetting all about it. Unfortunately, the poor victim can't always shake off the effects of the row in quite the same way. However, Arien cheerfulness, spontaneous generosity and kindness make them the greatest friends to have.

TAURUS
21st April to 21st May

These people are practical and persevering. Taureans are solid and reliable, regular in habits, sometimes a bit wet behind the ears and stubborn as mules. Their love of money and the comfort it can bring may make them very materialistic in outlook. They are most suited to a practical career which brings with it few surprises and plenty of money. However, they have a strong artistic streak which can be expressed in work, hobbies and interests.

Some Taureans are quick and clever, highly amusing and quite outrageous in appearance, but underneath this crazy exterior is a background of true talent and very hard work. This type may be a touch arrogant. Other Taureans hate to be rushed or hassled, preferring to work quietly and thoroughly at their own pace. They take relationships very seriously and make safe and reliable partners. They may keep their worries to themselves but they are not usually liars or sexually untrustworthy.

Being so very sensual as well as patient, these people make excellent lovers. Their biggest downfall comes later in life when they have a tendency to plonk themselves down in front of the television night after night, tuning out the rest of the world. Another problem with some Taureans is their 'pet hate', which they'll harp on about at any given opportunity. Their virtues are common sense, loyalty, responsibility and a pleasant, non-hostile approach to others. Taureans are much brighter than anyone gives them credit, and it is hard to beat them in an argument because they usually know what they are talking about. If a Taurean is on your side, they make wonderful friends and comfortable and capable colleagues.

GEMINI
22nd May to 21st June

Geminis are often accused of being short on intellect and unable to stick to anyone or anything for long. In a nutshell, great fun at a party but totally unreliable. This is unfair: nobody works harder, is more reliable or capable than Geminis when they put their mind to a task, especially if there is a chance of making large sums of money! Unfortunately, they have a low boredom threshold and they can drift away from something or someone when it no longer interests them. They like to be busy, with plenty of variety in their lives and the opportunity to communicate with others. Their forte lies in the communications industry where they shamelessly pinch ideas and improve on them. Many Geminis are highly ambitious people who won't allow anything or anyone to stand in their way.

They are surprisingly constant in relationships, often marrying for life but, if it doesn't work out, they will walk out and put the experience behind them. Geminis need relationships and if one fails, they will soon start looking for the next. Faithfulness is another story, however, because the famous Gemini curiosity can lead to any number of adventures. Geminis educate their children well while neglecting to see whether they have a clean shirt. The house is full of books, videos, televisions, CDs, newspapers and magazines and there is a phone in every room as well as in the car, the loo and the Gemini lady's handbag.

CANCER
22nd June to 23rd July

Cancerians look for security on the one hand and adventure and novelty on the other. They are popular because they really listen to what others are saying. Their own voices are attractive too. They are naturals for sales work and in any kind of advisory capacity. Where their own problems are concerned, they can disappear inside themselves and brood, which makes it hard for others to understand them. Cancerians spend a good deal of time worrying about their families and, even more so, about money. They appear soft but are very hard to influence.

Many Cancerians are small traders and many more work in teaching or the caring professions. They have a feel for history, perhaps collecting historical mementoes, and their memories are excellent. They need to have a home but they love to travel away from it, being happy in the knowledge that it is there waiting for them to come back to. There are a few Cancerians who seem to drift through life and expect other members of their family to keep them.

Romantically, they prefer to be settled and they fear being alone. A marriage would need to be really bad before they consider leaving, and if they do, they soon look for a new partner. These people can be scoundrels in business because they hate parting with money once they have their hands on it. However, their charm and intelligence usually manage to get them out of trouble.

LEO
24th July to 23rd August

Leos can be marvellous company or a complete pain in the neck. Under normal circumstances, they are warm-hearted, generous, sociable and popular but they can be very moody and irritable when under pressure or under the weather. Leos put their heart and soul into whatever they are doing and they can work like demons for a while. However, they cannot keep up the pace for long and they need to get away, zonk out on the sofa and take frequent holidays. These people always appear confident and they look like true winners, but their confidence can suddenly evaporate, leaving them unsure and unhappy with their efforts. They are extremely sensitive to hurt and they cannot take ridicule or even very much teasing.

Leos are proud. They have very high standards in all that they do and most have great integrity and honesty, but there are some who are complete and utter crooks. These people can stand on their dignity and be very snobbish. Their arrogance can become insufferable and they can take their powers of leadership into the realms of bossiness. They are convinced that they should be in charge and they can be very obstinate. Some Leos love the status and lifestyle which proclaims their successes. Many work in glamour professions such as the airline and entertainment industries. Others spend their day communing with computers and other high-tech gadgetry. In loving relationships, they are loyal but only while the magic lasts. If boredom sets in, they often start looking around for fresh fields. They are the most generous and loving of people and they need to play affectionately. Leos are kind, charming and they live life to the full.

VIRGO
24th August to 23rd September

Virgos are highly intelligent, interested in everything and everyone and happy to be busy with many jobs and hobbies. Many have some kind of specialized knowledge and most are good with their hands, but their nit-picking ways can infuriate colleagues. They find it hard to discuss their innermost feelings and this can make them hard to understand. In many ways, they are happier doing something practical than dealing with relationships. Virgos can also overdo the self-sacrificial bit and make themselves martyrs to other people's impractical lifestyles. They are willing to fit in with whatever is going on and can adjust to most things, but they mustn't neglect their own needs.

Although excellent communicators and wonderfully witty conversationalists, Virgos prefer to express their deepest feelings by actions rather than words. Most avoid touching all but very close friends and family members and many find lovey-dovey behaviour embarrassing. They can be very highly sexed and may use this as a way of expressing love. Virgos are criticized a good deal as children and are often made to feel unwelcome in their childhood homes. In turn, they become very critical of others and they can use this in order to wound.

Many Virgos overcome inhibitions by taking up acting, music, cookery or sports. Acting is particularly common to this sign because it allows them to put aside their fears and take on the mantle of someone quite different. They are shy and slow to make friends but when they do accept someone, they are the loyalest, gentlest and kindest of companions. They are great company and have a wonderful sense of humour.

LIBRA
24th September to 23rd October

Librans have a deceptive appearance, looking soft but being tough and quite selfish underneath. Astrological tradition tells us that this sign is dedicated to marriage, but a high proportion of them prefer to remain single, particularly when a difficult relationship comes to an end. These people are great to tell secrets to because they never listen to anything properly and promptly forget whatever is said. The confusion between their desire to co-operate with others and the need for self-expression is even more evident when at work. The best job is one where they are a part of an organization but able to take responsibility and make their own decisions.

While some Librans are shy and lacking in confidence, others are strong and determined with definite leadership qualities. All need to find a job that entails dealing with others and which does not wear out their delicate nerves. All Librans are charming, sophisticated and diplomatic, but can be confusing for others. All have a strong sense of justice and fair play but most haven't the strength to take on a determinedly lame duck. They project an image which is attractive, chosen to represent their sense of status and refinement. Being inclined to experiment sexually, they are not the most faithful of partners and even goody-goody Librans are terrible flirts.

SCORPIO
24th October to 22nd November

Reliable, resourceful and enduring, Scorpios seem to be the strong men and women of the zodiac. But are they really? They can be nasty at times, dishing out what they see as the truth, no matter how unwelcome. Their own feelings are sensitive and they are easily hurt, but they won't show any hurt or weakness in themselves to others. When they are very low or unhappy, this turns inwards, attacking their immune systems and making them ill. However, they have great resilience and they bounce back time and again from the most awful ailments.

Nobody needs to love and be loved more than a Scorpio, but their partners must stand up to them because they will give anyone they don't respect a very hard time indeed. They are the most loyal and honest of companions, both in personal relationships and at work. One reason for this is their hatred of change or uncertainty. Scorpios enjoy being the power behind the throne with someone else occupying the hot seat. This way, they can quietly manipulate everyone, set one against another and get exactly what they want from the situation.

Scorpios' voices are their best feature, often low, well-modulated and cultured and these wonderful voices are used to the full in pleasant persuasion. These people are neither as highly sexed nor as difficult as most astrology books make out, but they do have their passions (even if these are not always for sex itself) and they like to be thought of as sexy. They love to shock and to appear slightly dangerous, but they also make kind-hearted and loyal friends, superb hosts and gentle people who are often very fond of animals – in a nutshell, great people when they are not being cruel, stingy or devious!

SAGITTARIUS
23rd November to 21st December

Sagittarians are great company because they are interested in everything and everyone. Broad-minded and lacking in prejudice, they are fascinated by even the strangest of people. With their optimism and humour, they are often the life and soul of the party, while they are in a good mood. They can become quite down-hearted, crabby and awkward on occasion, but not usually for long. They can be hurtful to others because they cannot resist speaking what they see as the truth, even if it causes embarrassment. However, their tactlessness is usually innocent and they have no desire to hurt.

Sagittarians need an unconventional lifestyle, preferably one which allows them to travel. They cannot be cooped up in a cramped environment and they need to meet new people and to explore a variety of ideas during their day's work. Money is not their god and they will work for a pittance if they feel inspired by the task. Their values are spiritual rather than material. Many are attracted to the spiritual side of life and may be interested in the Church, philosophy, astrology and other New Age subjects. Higher education and legal matters attract them because these subjects expand and explore intellectual boundaries. Long-lived relationships may not appeal because they need to feel free and unfettered, but they can do well with a self-sufficient and independent partner. Despite all this intellectualism and need for freedom, Sagittarians have a deep need to be cuddled and touched and they need to be supported emotionally.

AQUARIUS
21st January to 19th February

Clever, friendly, kind and humane, Aquarians are the easiest people to make friends with but probably the hardest to really know. They are often more comfortable with acquaintances than with those who are close to them. Being dutiful, they would never let a member of their family go without their basic requirements, but they can be strangely, even deliberately, blind to their underlying needs and real feelings. They are more comfortable with causes and their idealistic ideas than with the day-to-day routine of family life. Their homes may reflect this lack of interest by being rather messy, although there are other Aquarians who are almost clinically house proud.

Their opinions are formed early in life and are firmly fixed. Being patient with people, they make good teachers and are, themselves, always willing to learn something new. But are they willing to go out and earn a living? Some are, many are not. These people can be extremely eccentric in the way they dress or the way they live. They make a point of being 'different' and they can actually feel very unsettled and uneasy if made to conform, even outwardly. Their restless, sceptical minds mean that they need an alternative kind of lifestyle which stretches them mentally.

In relationships, they are surprisingly constant and faithful and they only stray when they know in their hearts that there is no longer anything to be gained from staying put. Aquarians are often very attached to the first real commitment in their lives and they can even remarry a previously divorced partner. Their sexuality fluctuates, perhaps peaking for some years then pushed aside while something else occupies their energies, then high again. Many Aquarians are extremely highly sexed and very clever and active in bed.

PISCES
20th February to 20th March

This idealistic, dreamy, kind and impractical sign needs a lot of understanding. They have a fractured personality which has so many sides and so many moods that they probably don't even understand themselves. Nobody is more kind, thoughtful and caring, but they have a tendency to drift away from people and responsibilities. When the going gets rough, they get going! Being creative, clever and resourceful, these people can achieve a great deal and really reach the top, but few of them do. Some Pisceans have a self-destruct button which they press before reaching their goal. Others do achieve success and the motivating force behind this essentially spiritual and mystical sign is often money. Many Pisceans feel insecure, most suffer some experience of poverty at some time in their early lives and they grow into adulthood determined that they will never feel that kind of uncertainty again.

Pisceans are at home in any kind of creative or caring career. Many can be found in teaching, nursing and the arts. Some find life hard and are often unhappy; many have to make tremendous sacrifices on behalf of others. This may be a pattern which repeats itself from childhood, where the message is that the Piscean's needs always come last. These people can be stubborn, awkward, selfish and quite nasty when a friendship or relationship goes sour. This is because, despite their basically kind and gentle personality, there is a side which needs to be in charge of any relationship. Pisceans make extremely faithful partners as long as the romance doesn't evaporate and their partners treat them well. Problems occur if they are mistreated or rejected, if they become bored or restless or if their alcohol intake climbs over the danger level. The Piscean lover is a sexual fantasist, so in this sphere of life anything can happen!

CAPRICORN

You and Yours

What is it like to bring up an Arien child? What kind of father does a Libran make? How does it feel to grow up with a Sagittarian mother? Whatever your own sign is, how do you appear to your parents and how do you behave towards your children?

THE CAPRICORN FATHER

These are true family men who cope with housework and child-rearing but they are sometimes too involved in work to spend much time at home. Dutiful and caring, these men are unlikely to run off with a bimbo or to leave their family wanting. However, they can be stuffy or out of touch with the younger generation. They encourage their children to do well and to behave properly.

THE CAPRICORN MOTHER

Capricorn women make good mothers but they may be inclined to fuss. Being ambitious, they want their children to do well and they teach them to respect teachers, youth leaders and so on. These mothers usually find work outside the home in order to supplement the family income. They are very loving but they can be too keen on discipline and the careful management of pocket money.

THE CAPRICORN CHILD

Capricorn children are little adults from the day they are born. They don't need much discipline or encouragement to do well at school. Modest and well behaved, they are almost too good to be true. However, they suffer badly with their nerves and can be prone to ailments such as asthma. They need to be taught to let go, have fun and enjoy their childhood. Some are too selfish or ambitious to make friends.

THE ARIES FATHER

Arien men take the duties of fatherhood very seriously. They read to their children, take them on educational trips and expose them to art and music from an early age. They can push their children too hard or tyrannize the sensitive ones. The Aries father wants his children not only to have what he didn't have but also to be what he isn't. He respects those children who are high achievers and who can stand up to him.

THE ARIES MOTHER

Arien women love their children dearly and will make amazing sacrifices for them, but don't expect them to give up their jobs or their outside interests for motherhood. Competitive herself, this mother wants her children to be the best and she may push them too hard. However, she is kind-hearted, affectionate and not likely to over-discipline them. She treats her offspring as adults and is well loved in return.

THE ARIES CHILD

Arien children are hard to ignore. Lively, noisy and demanding, they try to enjoy every moment of their childhood. Despite this, they lack confidence and need reassurance. Often clever but lacking in self-discipline, they need to be made to attend school each day and to do their homework. Active and competitive, these children excel in sports, dancing or learning to play a pop music instrument.

THE TAURUS FATHER

This man cares deeply for his children and wants the best for them, but doesn't expect the impossible. He may lay the law down and he can be unsympathetic to the attitudes and interests of a new generation. He may frighten young children by shouting at them. Being a responsible parent, he offers a secure family base but he may find it hard to let them go when they want to leave.

THE TAURUS MOTHER

These women make good mothers due to their highly domesticated nature. Some are real earth mothers, baking bread and making wonderful toys and games for their children. Sane and sensible but not highly imaginative, they do best with a child who has ordinary needs and they get confused by those who are 'special' in any way. Taurus mothers are very loving but they use reasonable discipline when necessary.

THE TAURUS CHILD

Taurean children can be surprisingly demanding. Their loud voices and stubborn natures can be irritating. Plump, sturdy and strong, some are shy and retiring, while others can bully weaker children. Artistic, sensual and often musical, these children can lose themselves in creative or beautiful hobbies. They need to be encouraged to share and express love and also to avoid too many sweet foods.

CAPRICORN

THE GEMINI FATHER

Gemini fathers are fairly laid back in their approach and, while they cope well with fatherhood, they can become bored with home life and try to escape from their duties. Some are so absorbed with work that they hardly see their offspring. At home, Gemini fathers will provide books, educational toys and as much computer equipment as the child can use, and they enjoy a family game of tennis.

THE GEMINI MOTHER

These mothers can be very pushy because they see education as the road to success. They encourage a child to pursue any interest and will sacrifice time and money for this. They usually have a job outside the home and may rely on other people to do some child-minding for them. Their children cannot always count on coming home to a balanced meal, but they can talk to their mothers on any subject.

THE GEMINI CHILD

These children needs a lot of reassurance because they often feel like square pegs in round holes. They either do very well at school and incur the wrath of less able children, or they fail dismally and have to make it up later in life. They learn to read early and some have excellent mechanical ability while others excel at sports. They get bored very easily and they can be extremely irritating.

THE CANCER FATHER

A true family man who will happily embrace even stepchildren as if they were his own. Letting go of the family when they grow up is another matter. Cancerian sulks, moodiness and bouts of childishness can confuse or frighten some children, while his changeable attitude to money can make them unsure of what they should ask for. This father enjoys domesticity and child-rearing and he may be happy to swap roles.

THE CANCER MOTHER

Cancerian women are excellent home makers and cheerful and reasonable mothers, as long as they have a part-time job or an interest outside the house. They instinctively know when a child is unhappy and can deal with it in a manner which is both efficient and loving. These women have a reputation for clinging but most are quite realistic when the time comes for their brood to leave the nest.

THE CANCER CHILD

These children are shy, cautious and slow to grow up. They may achieve little at school, 'disappearing' behind louder and more demanding classmates. They can be worriers who complain about every ache and pain or suffer from imaginary fears. They may take on the mother's role in the family, dictating to their sisters and brothers at times. Gentle and loving but moody and secretive, they need a lot of love and encouragement.

THE LEO FATHER

These men can be wonderful fathers as long as they remember that children are not simply small and rather obstreperous adults. Leo fathers like to be involved with their children and encourage them to do well at school. They happily make sacrifices for their children and they truly want them to have the best, but they can be a bit too strict and they may demand too high a standard.

THE LEO MOTHER

Leo mothers are very caring and responsible but they cannot be satisfied with a life of pure domesticity, and need to combine motherhood with a job. These mothers don't fuss about minor details. They're prepared to put up with a certain amount of noise and disruption, but they can be irritable and they may demand too much of their children.

THE LEO CHILD

These children know almost from the day they are born that they are special. They are usually loved and wanted but they are also aware that a lot is expected from them. Leo children appear outgoing but they are surprisingly sensitive and easily hurt. They only seem to wake up to the need to study a day or so after they leave school, but they find a way to make a success of their lives.

THE VIRGO FATHER

These men may be embarrassed by open declarations of love and affection and find it hard to give cuddles and reassurance to small children. Yet they love their offspring dearly and will go to any lengths to see that they have the best possible education and outside activities. Virgoan men can become wrapped up in their work, forgetting to spend time relaxing and playing with their children.

THE VIRGO MOTHER

Virgoan women try hard to be good mothers because they probably had a poor childhood themselves. They love their children very much and want the best for them but they may be fussy about unnecessary details, such as dirt on the kitchen floor or the state of the children's school books. If they can keep their tensions and longings away from their children, they can be the most kindly and loving parents.

THE VIRGO CHILD

Virgoan children are practical and capable and can do very well at school, but they are not always happy. They don't always fit in and they may have difficulty making friends. They may be shy, modest and sensitive and they can find it hard to live up to their own impossibly high standards. Virgo children don't need harsh discipline, they want approval and will usually respond perfectly well to reasoned argument.

THE LIBRA FATHER

Libran men mean well, but they may not actually perform that well. They have no great desire to be fathers but welcome their children when they come along. They may slide out of the more irksome tasks by having an absorbing job or a series of equally absorbing hobbies which keep them occupied outside the home. These men do better with older children because they can talk to them.

THE LIBRA MOTHER

Libran mothers are pleasant and easy-going but some of them are more interested in their looks, their furnishings and their friends than their children. Others are very loving and kind but a bit too soft, which results in their children disrespecting them or walking all over them in later life. These mothers enjoy talking to their children and encouraging them to succeed.

THE LIBRA CHILD

These children are charming and attractive and they have no difficulty in getting on with people. They make just enough effort to get through school and only do the household jobs they cannot dodge. They may drive their parents mad with their demands for the latest gadget or gimmick. However, their common sense, sense of humour and reasonable attitude makes harsh discipline unnecessary.

THE SCORPIO FATHER

These fathers can be really awful or absolutely wonderful, and there aren't any half-measures. Good Scorpio men provide love and security because they stick closely to their homes and families and are unlikely to do a disappearing act. Difficult ones can be loud and tyrannical. These proud men want their children to be the best.

THE SCORPIO MOTHER

These mothers are either wonderful or not really maternal at all, although they try to do their best. If they take to child-rearing, they encourage their offspring educationally and in their hobbies. These mothers have no time for whiny or miserable children but they respect outgoing, talented and courageous ones, and can cope with a handful.

THE SCORPIO CHILD

Scorpio children are competitive, self-centred and unwilling to co-operate with brothers, sisters, teachers or anyone else when in an awkward mood. They can be deeply unreadable, living in a world of their own and filled with all kinds of strange angry feelings. At other times, they can be delightfully caring companions. They love animals, sports, children's organizations and group activities.

THE SAGITTARIUS FATHER

Sagittarian fathers will give their children all the education they can stand. They happily provide books, equipment and take their offspring out to see anything interesting. They may not always be available to their offspring, but they make up for it by surprising their families with tickets for sporting events or by bringing home a pet for the children. These men are cheerful and childlike themselves.

THE SAGITTARIUS MOTHER

This mother is kind, easy-going and pleasant. She may be very ordinary with suburban standards or she may be unbelievably eccentric, forcing the family to take up strange diets and filling the house with weird and wonderful people. Some opt out of child-rearing by finding childminders while others take on other people's children and a host of animals in addition to their own.

THE SAGITTARIUS CHILD

Sagittarian children love animals and the outdoor life but they are just as interested in sitting around and watching the telly as the next child. These children have plenty of friends whom they rush out and visit at every opportunity. Happy and optimistic but highly independent, they cannot be pushed in any direction. Many leave home in late their teens in order to travel.

THE AQUARIAN FATHER

Some Aquarian men have no great desire to be fathers but they make a reasonable job of it when they have to. They cope best when their children are reasonable and intelligent but, if they are not, they tune out and ignore them. Some Aquarians will spend hours inventing games and toys for their children while all of them value education and try to push their children.

THE AQUARIAN MOTHER

Some of these mothers are too busy putting the world to rights to see what is going on in their own family. However, they are kind, reasonable and keen on education. They may be busy outside the house but they often take their children along with them. They are not fussy homemakers, and are happy to have all the neighbourhood kids in the house. They respect a child's dignity.

THE AQUARIAN CHILD

These children may be demanding when very young but they become much more reasonable when at school. They are easily bored and need outside interests. They have many friends and may spend more time in other people's homes than in their own. Very stubborn and determined, they make it quite clear from an early age that they intend to do things their own way. These children suffer from nerves.

THE PISCES FATHER

Piscean men fall into one of two categories. Some are kind and gentle, happy to take their children on outings and to introduce them to art, culture, music or sport. Others are disorganized and unpredictable. The kindly fathers don't always push their children. They encourage their kids to have friends and a pet or two.

THE PISCES MOTHER

Piscean mothers may be lax and absent-minded but they love their children and are usually loved in return. Many are too disorganized to run a perfect household so meals, laundry, etc. can be hit and miss, but their children prosper despite this, although many learn to reverse the mother/child roles. These mothers teach their offspring to appreciate animals and the environment.

THE PISCES CHILD

These sensitive children may find life difficult and they can get lost among stronger, more demanding brothers and sisters. They may drive their parents batty with their dreamy attitude and they can make a fuss over nothing. They need a secure and loving home with parents who shield them from harsh reality while encouraging them to develop their imaginative and psychic abilities.

CAPRICORN

Your Rising Sign

WHAT IS A RISING SIGN?
Your rising sign is the sign of the zodiac which was climbing up over the eastern horizon the moment you were born. This is not the same as your Sun sign; your Sun sign depends upon your date of birth, but your rising sign depends upon the time of day that you were born, combined with your date and place of birth.

The rising sign modifies your Sun sign character quite considerably, so when you have worked out which is your rising sign, read pages 39–40 to see how it modifies your Sun sign. Then take a deeper look by going back to 'All the Other Sun Signs' on page 21 and read the relevant Sun sign material there to discover more about your ascendant (rising sign) nature.

One final point is that the sign that is opposite your rising sign (or 'ascendant') is known as your 'descendant'. This shows what you want from other people, and it may give a clue as to your choice of friends, colleagues and lovers (see pages 41–3). So once you have found your rising sign and read the character interpretation, check out the character reading for your descendant to see what you are looking for in others.

How to Begin

Read through this section while following the example below. Even if you only have a vague idea of your birth time, you won't find this method difficult; just go for a rough time of birth and then read the Sun sign information for that sign to see if it fits your personality. If you seem to be more like the sign that comes before or after it, then it is likely that you were born a little earlier or later than your assumed time of birth. Don't forget to deduct an hour for summertime births.

1. Look at the illustration top right. You will notice that it has the time of day arranged around the outer circle. It looks a bit like a clock face, but it is different because it shows the whole 24-hour day in two-hour blocks.

2. Write the astrological symbol that represents the Sun (a circle with a dot in the middle) in the segment that corresponds to your time of birth. (If you were born during Daylight Saving or British Summer Time, deduct one hour from your birth time.) Our example shows someone who was born between 2 a.m. and 4 a.m.

CAPRICORN

3. Now write the name of your sign or the symbol for your sign on the line which is at the end of the block of time that your Sun falls into. Our example shows a person who was born between 2 a.m. and 4 a.m. under the sign of Pisces.

4. Either write in the names of the zodiac signs or use the symbols in their correct order (see the key below) around the chart in an anti-clockwise direction, starting from the line which is at the start of the block of time that your sun falls into.

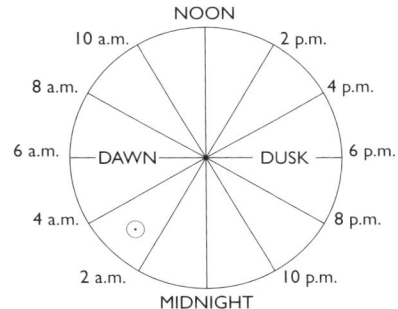

5. The sign that appears on the left-hand side of the wheel at the 'Dawn' line is your rising sign, or ascendant. The example shows a person born with the Sun in Pisces and with Aquarius rising. Incidentally, the example chart also shows Leo, which falls on the 'Dusk' line, in the descendant. You will always find the ascendant sign on the 'Dawn' line and the descendant sign on the 'Dusk' line.

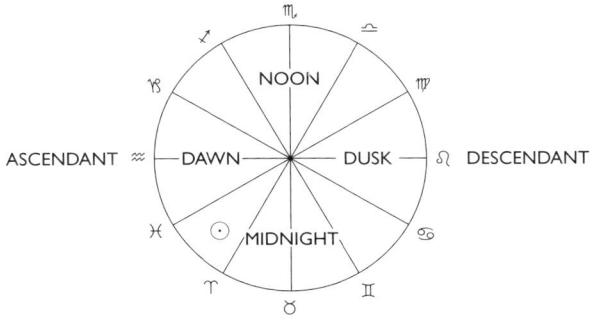

♈ Aries	♋ Cancer	♎ Libra	♑ Capricorn
♉ Taurus	♌ Leo	♏ Scorpio	♒ Aquarius
♊ Gemini	♍ Virgo	♐ Sagittarius	♓ Pisces

CAPRICORN

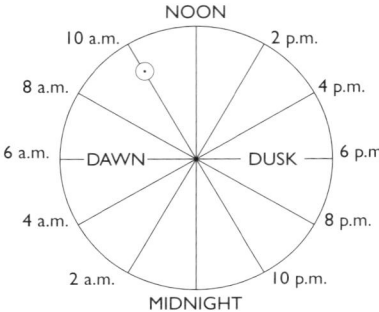

Here is another example for you to run through, just to make sure that you have grasped the idea correctly. This example is for a more awkward time of birth, being exactly on the line between two different blocks of time. This example is for a person with a Capricorn Sun sign who was born at 10 a.m.

1. The Sun is placed exactly on the 10 a.m. line.

2. The sign of Capricorn is placed on the 10 a.m. line.

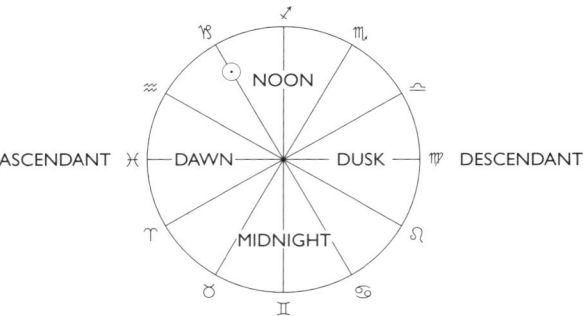

3. All the other signs are placed in astrological order (anti-clockwise) around the chart.

4. This person has the Sun in Capricorn and Pisces rising, and therefore with Virgo on the descendant.

Using the Rising Sign Finder

Please bear in mind that this method is approximate. If you want to be really sure of your rising sign, you should contact an astrologer. However, this system will work with reasonable accuracy wherever you were born. Check out the Sun and ascendant combination in the following pages. Once you've done so, if you're not quite sure you've got it right, you should also read the Sun sign character readings on pages 21–8 for the signs both before and after the rising sign you think is yours. Rising signs are such an obvious part of one's personality that one quick glance will show you which one belongs to you.

Can Your Rising Sign Tell You More about Your Future?

When it comes to tracking events, the rising sign is equal in importance to the Sun sign. So, if you want a more accurate forecast when reading newspapers or magazines, you should read the horoscope for your rising sign as well as your Sun sign. In the case of books such as this, you should really treat yourself to two: one to correspond with your rising sign, and another for your usual Sun sign, and read both each day!

How Your Rising Sign Modifies Your Sun Sign

CAPRICORN WITH ARIES RISING This powerful combination makes for a top politician or a captain of industry. However, your home and family are also very important to you.

CAPRICORN WITH TAURUS RISING You are extremely sensual and probably quite artistic. You may be keen on cooking, gardening, music, dancing or any practical application of creative ideas.

CAPRICORN WITH GEMINI RISING You may live for work and forget to have a personal life. However, you have a lively sense of humour and you are a wonderful communicator.

CAPRICORN WITH CANCER RISING This gentle combination makes

CAPRICORN

you a great family member. You are more ambitious than you look, and you want your family to get on in life.

CAPRICORN WITH LEO RISING Work is important to you, but you also enjoy your family and social life. You are more outgoing than the average Capricorn. You could be keen on alternative health matters.

CAPRICORN WITH VIRGO RISING You have a great sense of humour which probably saves you from being too serious. You are capable of doing very detailed work, and anything to do with health and healing appeals to you.

CAPRICORN WITH LIBRA RISING This combination could make you a business whiz-kid or simply the power behind somebody else's throne. You can use your artistic talent in practical ways.

CAPRICORN WITH SCORPIO RISING You could be an aggressive money-maker with executive abilities. However, you are equally interested in music, literature and what makes the world tick.

CAPRICORN WITH SAGITTARIUS RISING You are more outgoing than the average Capricorn, with a sense of adventure and a fondness for travel and meeting new and interesting people.

CAPRICORN WITH CAPRICORN RISING This is Capricorn in its purest form, therefore you are hard-working, patient, thorough and capable of coping with details. You probably had a hard or lonely childhood. You would be more introverted if born after dawn than if you were born before.

CAPRICORN WITH AQUARIUS RISING This unusual combination makes you sensitive, intuitive and interested in New Age ideas. You may have had a lonely childhood, not fitting in at school or at home.

CAPRICORN WITH PISCES RISING You enjoy making friends and may run some kind of social club. You are sensitive, rather psychic and quite gentle. However, your mind is very quick and you have a good sense of humour.

Capricorn in Love

YOU NEED:

STABILITY You cannot cope with a flighty partner because you need stability and continuity in your relationships. You appreciate a partner who works hard and who sticks at what they do.

KINDNESS You are kind and considerate yourself and you will do anything to make your partner feel comfortable and happy. You do your best to cheer up a sick or downhearted partner.

LOVE The chances are that you had a rather hard childhood and you need the constant reassurance that you are worthy of love and that you are still desirable.

YOU GIVE:

DEPTH You are surprisingly passionate when you are comfortably settled in a deep and meaningful relationship. You feel deeply about life and you want your partner to be as sincere about life and love as you are.

RESPONSIBILITY You don't take your responsibilities lightly and you spend your earnings wisely. You are not lazy or a big spender and you take care of those whom you love through all kinds of trials and tribulations. You have a fairly serious attitude to life.

LOYALTY You are not the kind to run off with someone else on a whim. You take your relationship seriously and you stand by your partner against all odds.

WHAT YOU CAN EXPECT FROM THE OTHER ZODIAC SIGNS:

ARIES *Truth, honesty, playfulness*. You can expect an open and honest relationship with no hidden agendas. Your Arien lover will be a bit childish at times, however.

TAURUS *Security, stability, comfort.* Taureans will stand by you and try to improve your financial position. They will create a beautiful homes and gardens for their partners.

GEMINI *Stimulation, encouragement, variety.* Gemini lovers are never boring; they give encouragement and are always ready for an outing. They give emotional support too.

CANCER *Emotional security, companionship. help.* Cancerians will never leave you stranded at a party or alone when suffering from the flu. They always lend a hand when asked.

CAPRICORN

LEO *Affection, fun, loyalty.* Leo lovers are very steadfast and they would avenge anyone who hurt one of their family. They enjoy romping and playing affectionate love games.

VIRGO *Clear-thinking, kindness, humour.* Virgoans make intelligent and amusing partners. They can be critical but are never unkind. They take their responsibility towards you seriously.

LIBRA *Fair-play, sensuality, advice.* Librans will listen to your problems and give balanced and sensible advice. They are wonderfully inventive, and are affectionate lovers too.

SCORPIO *Truth, passion, loyalty.* Scorpios will take your interests as seriously as they do their own. They will stick by you when the going gets tough and they won't flannel you.

SAGITTARIUS *Honesty, fun, novelty.* Theses lovers will never bore you and they'll keep up with whatever pace you set. They seek the truth and they don't keep their feelings hidden.

AQUARIUS *Stimulation, friendship, sexuality.* Aquarians are friends as well as lovers. They are great fun because you never know what they are going to do next, in or out of bed.

PISCES *Sympathy, support, love.* These romantic lovers never let you down. They can take you with them into their personal fantasy world and they are always ready for a laugh.

WHICH SIGN ARE YOU COMPATIBLE WITH?

CAPRICORN/ARIES
Sparky but quite successful combination.

CAPRICORN/TAURUS
Could be very happy and comfortable together.

CAPRICORN/GEMINI
This could work well, both personally and in business.

CAPRICORN/CANCER
An excellent combination as both are keen on money and family.

CAPRICORN/LEO
Capricorn may appear too slow for Leo but this can work.

CAPRICORN/VIRGO
Capricorn could encourage Virgo and Virgo inspire Capricorn.

CAPRICORN/LIBRA
A bit competitive, especially in business, but fairly good.

CAPRICORN/SCORPIO
Can work well, as Scorpio will understand Capricorn's ambition.

CAPRICORN

CAPRICORN/SAGITTARIUS
Either excellent or simply no good at all.

CAPRICORN/CAPRICORN
Too similar for comfort, or happy to be alike.

CAPRICORN/AQUARIUS
Shared interests could make this successful.

CAPRICORN/PISCES
Pisces could be too dreamy and idealistic for Capricorn.

Your Prospects for 1999

LOVE

Fancy-free Capricorns have a fairly good chance of meeting someone new this year because, although there could be better auguries for love and romance, there could also be worse ones. Venus is in the area of your chart that is devoted to romance during late March and early April and this will help you to appear more attractive to the opposite sex although it will probably be from June to August that anything settled and secure comes along. July and August look like wonderful times to meet a new lover, especially if you do so while travelling or engaging on some leisure pursuit. After that, things quieten down a bit and you may even become quite unsure of your own feelings or those of your lover until the last couple of months of the year. Settled Capricorns should have an easier time of it this year than for many years past. The only time when even the most minor problem would ruffle the calm of your relationship would be during the second half of July and the first week of August. To be honest, even this blot on the horizon is more likely to be due to a financial or business muddle than any kind of romantic problem. There may be some financial setbacks for you and your lover during August but if you take a sensible attitude and both hold back on your spending for a while, this won't cause you too much hassle.

MONEY AND WORK

Capricorns usually put a lot of effort into their job and they are thorough and conscientious in all they do. This year, there should be nothing to stop you enjoying your working life to the full and there are indications that you could reach a very high position before the year is over. You will find male colleagues helpful and one in particular will have a great deal of faith in your abilities, thereby encouraging you to reach for the stars. You can achieve a great deal now. As far as your own personal finances are concerned, this will be an up-and-down year. Sure, you may earn good money but you will be beset by a number of large expenses and some of these may be unexpected and unpredictable. The very end of the year will be a better time for you but there is still evidence that your level of spending will be high. Other people will let you down over money matters so try not to lend money or to become involved in get-rich-quick schemes that are put to you by others this year. The most awkward times of the year for your finances are January, February, July and August because, apart from a number of planetary events that will occur at that time, there are also eclipses of the Sun and of the Moon to contend with. Eclipses always bring unexpected shocks and in your case these are likely to affect your pocket.

HEALTH

This is an area of your life that will need to be watched a little this year. There are no indications of severe health problems but there could be some setbacks from June to August when a couple of planets are in retrograde motion opposite the area of your chart that affects your health. However, you should be feeling fit and well earlier in the year and also during the latter part of the year. There is no clear indication of the area of your body that should be coddled but it would be as well to make sure that you wear well-fitting shoes and that you avoid strappy or loose sandals that could let your feet and ankles down. If you want to begin a diet or fitness regime, do so during April and May when your will power will be at its best.

FAMILY AND HOME

There is evidence that you could make changes in your domestic circumstances this year and a move of house could be on the cards for you now. If you do make such changes, the chances are that you will make money on the deal while at the same time making your home life more comfortable. If renovations, property dealings or anything of the kind go slowly during the first couple of months of 1999, this will be compensated for by the speed at which things happen shortly after this. Family life will be pretty good now and parents especially will be happy to give you a hand in any way that you want for much of the year.

CAPRICORN

LUCK

Home is where the heart is this year and it is also where your luck is. You hardly have to move out of the door to be lucky. A kind offer from a friend may lead to an unexpected trip during July and if you take this offer up, you will have a wonderful time. Other people could put a good word or two your way, especially at work at times, but a series of lucky breaks could come as a result of being a member of a club or society.

The Aspects and their Astrological Meanings

CONJUNCT	This shows important events which are usually, but not always, good.
SEXTILE	Good, particularly for work and mental activity.
SQUARE	Difficult, challenging.
TRINE	Great for romance, family life and creativity.
OPPOSITE	Awkward, depressing, challenging.
INTO	This shows when a particular planet enters a new sign of the zodiac, thus setting off a new phase or a new set of circumstances.
DIRECT	When a planet resumes normal direct motion.
RETROGRADE	When a planet apparently begins to go backwards.
VOID	When the Moon makes no aspect to any planet.

CAPRICORN

September at a Glance

LOVE	♥	♥	♥	♥	
WORK	★	★			
MONEY	£	£	£	£	£
HEALTH	✪	✪	✪		
LUCK	♘	♘	♘	♘	♘

TUESDAY, 1ST SEPTEMBER
Moon trine Saturn

Common sense rules the day as the Moon makes a positive contact with Saturn. Not for you airy-fairy flights of fancy. Your feet are planted firmly on the ground and you won't have much time for sentiment.

WEDNESDAY, 2ND SEPTEMBER
Void Moon

The term 'void of course' means that neither the Moon nor any of the other planets is making any important aspects during the course of their travels today. When this kind of day occurs, the worst thing you can do is to try to start something new or get anything important off the ground. Do nothing special today except for routine tasks.

THURSDAY, 3RD SEPTEMBER
Moon conjunct Neptune

It's a day to drift and dream, because the Moon is in contact with Neptune, refining your tastes and keeping you away from anything brash or vulgar. Take time to listen to music and indulge in a couple of fantasies. Escapism is wonderful in small doses!

FRIDAY, 4TH SEPTEMBER
Mars opposite Uranus

Something may happen today that makes you doubt yourself. Your values may be questioned, making you wonder if you are right after all. A friend may try to manipulate you into benefiting them, rather than you.

CAPRICORN

SATURDAY, 5TH SEPTEMBER
Moon opposite Venus

It's always easy to stir your sympathies, but the time comes when even you must admit that enough is enough. You seem to be surrounded by people who take your goodwill for granted and treat you as though you're a never-ending source of cash. Call a halt to this constant drain on your resources, or you'll have cause to regret it.

SUNDAY, 6TH SEPTEMBER
Full Moon eclipse

Today's eclipse shows that you feel the call of the new and the different in your life. Your ideas have changed but old habits still linger on, so if you want to make a break for freedom then this is the day to make a start. An outworn lifestyle cannot compete against your desire for knowledge and adventure. Take some action now!

MONDAY, 7TH SEPTEMBER
Moon sextile Neptune

With the Moon aspecting the ethereal Neptune a bolt from the blue, such as a sudden inspiration, will strike you today. Like the proverbial light-bulb, your brain will be illuminated by a brilliant idea!

TUESDAY, 8TH SEPTEMBER
Mercury into Virgo

Mercury enters the most philosophical area of your chart, giving you a chance to grow mentally. Many of your past beliefs will now fall by the wayside as you find other concepts that fit more logically into your life. Positive thinking is important now since you'll realize that it's only negativity that's held you back. The academically inclined should do well under this influence, and the tiny planet also gives a boost to your travel prospects.

WEDNESDAY, 9TH SEPTEMBER
Mercury trine Saturn

A chat with someone older or wiser would be advisable today. You may want to talk over some kind of technicality in connection with one of your hobbies or interests. Alternatively, there may be a few problems of a more serious nature that need to be aired.

CAPRICORN

THURSDAY, 10TH SEPTEMBER
Venus trine Saturn

There's a touch of heartache about today's stars, even though Saturn and Venus are in good aspect to each other. It may be that, although there's nothing seriously wrong, you may be unavoidably separated from a loved one for a while.

FRIDAY, 11TH SEPTEMBER
Mercury conjunct Venus

You are the soul of charm and tact today, and you could even manage to be quite outspoken without treading on anyone else's toes. You may fancy visiting a historic or educational spot, or even popping into a church to enjoy a service.

SATURDAY, 12TH SEPTEMBER
Moon sextile Mars

Work today will be your forte, because anything to do with chores and duties is likely to be very successful. Home-based duties will go well today too, so get down to the ironing or clearing out the garage because you'll feel all the better for doing so.

SUNDAY, 13TH SEPTEMBER
Moon square Jupiter

We hope you made the most of yesterday, because you may feel a bit under the weather today, making it hard to get through your usual chores. There may be trouble and uncertainty at work and you could feel that you are doing far more than you're being paid for. In short, you are suffering from the classic 'overworked and underpaid' syndrome. So what's new?

MONDAY, 14TH SEPTEMBER
Moon sextile Venus

You will be more at ease with yourself today than for some time past. You may have been overdoing it, perhaps trying too hard to reach a particular objective. Fair enough; you're in an ambitious frame of mind and there is something you want to achieve, but today you're being told to put this on to the back burner and give your nerves a rest.

TUESDAY, 15TH SEPTEMBER
Moon sextile Sun

This is a good day to get out and about, especially if you are in the company of someone you love. Even the most mundane journey can become a voyage of discovery, reawakening some of the old magic in your relationship.

CAPRICORN

WEDNESDAY, 16TH SEPTEMBER
Sun opposite Jupiter

This is not the day to take a chance on anything, because gambles of any kind will just not pay off now. Travelling, particularly visiting new places, is not auspicious either, we're afraid. If you must make a trip somewhere, prepare yourself for delays or disruptions and, if possible, make alternative arrangements for your journey.

THURSDAY, 17TH SEPTEMBER
Moon conjunct Mars

Passions run high when the Moon contacts Mars in the most intimate area of your chart. Of course there are many sorts of passion, so recognize that you're quite moody now and don't give in to feelings of jealousy. Sexual issues are very strong, so beware of infatuations and sudden enthusiasms because the appeal isn't likely to last.

FRIDAY, 18TH SEPTEMBER
Moon trine Saturn

The going gets easier and parental figures and people in positions of authority will prove to be very helpful today. If you are experiencing difficulties in a creative project, ask an expert for advice.

SATURDAY, 19TH SEPTEMBER
Mercury opposite Jupiter

Mercury rules short journeys and also local travel; Jupiter rules long-distance travel and exploration. These opposing planets are badly placed in your chart at the moment. The message, therefore, is don't travel unless you absolutely need to.

SUNDAY, 20TH SEPTEMBER
New Moon

Today's New Moon certainly indicates a new start for you. You're filled to the brim with good ideas and your mind is working overtime, bringing you close to genius level! If there's a subject that has interested you for some time, this could be your chance to learn more, and possibly gain a qualification. Educational matters are favoured now, as indeed is anything that increases your knowledge and experience. A stimulating conversation will point the way forward.

MONDAY, 21ST SEPTEMBER
Moon sextile Pluto

A little forethought will go a long way to solving problems before they become a

CAPRICORN

major issue. Think before you act, that's the celestial message of the Moon-Pluto aspect today. Haste will cause no end of mistakes, so why take the risk when you can work out your moves in advance? Save yourself time and trouble.

TUESDAY, 22ND SEPTEMBER
Sun trine Neptune

You simply long to escape from all the problems and pressures that are surrounding you and today there will be an opportunity to do just that. Take a walk by the seaside or in the country now and enjoy the fresh air and freedom.

WEDNESDAY, 23RD SEPTEMBER
Sun into Libra

Career affairs are highlighted, so concentrate on where you are going and make an effort to impress the right people over the next few weeks. Forget about romance for a while and focus on business and financial goals instead.

THURSDAY, 24TH SEPTEMBER
Mercury into Libra

Today, Mercury enters your Solar tenth house of aims and ambitions. You can now keep your eye fixed on your goals and know that you have a fair chance of achieving them. Concentrate on planning and strategy to make your dreams come true.

FRIDAY, 25TH SEPTEMBER
Sun conjunct Mercury

A father figure may be especially helpful to you or, alternatively, an authority figure will offer you good advice and a helping hand. Your mind is full of great ideas and fortunately the world seems keen to listen. You could even find yourself on the radio, on television or being quoted in the papers soon!

SATURDAY, 26TH SEPTEMBER
Moon conjunct Pluto

The Moon meets up with Pluto in the deepest, most mysterious recesses of your chart today. This means that your unconscious mind has an urgent message for you that you'd be unwise to ignore. A potent dream should be noted, as it may contain the answer to a problem that's been troubling you.

SUNDAY, 27TH SEPTEMBER
Mercury sextile Pluto

You may be full of great business ideas today, but you will need to look a little

CAPRICORN

deeper before putting them into action. There may also be something going on behind the scenes at work that, when revealed, will be beneficial.

MONDAY, 28TH SEPTEMBER
Moon trine Saturn

Any creative project that you have been working on will begin to fall into place. You may decide to take an interest in music or other artistic pursuits from now on, so sign on at your local college for those guitar lessons!

TUESDAY, 29TH SEPTEMBER
Sun sextile Pluto

Ideas that you've put on the back burner can now be reconsidered. For example, this would be a good time to turn a hobby into a money-making venture or to discover talents that you rarely put to good use.

WEDNESDAY, 30TH SEPTEMBER
Venus into Libra

A woman could be instrumental in helping you achieve one of your most deeply held ambitions today and, what is more, this offer could come completely out of the blue. This friend or colleague will put herself out for no reason other than to foster your talent. A sudden and unexpected social invitation could come through work now, and this is so favourable that you really must accept.

October at a Glance

LOVE	❤	❤	❤	
WORK	★	★	★	
MONEY	£			
HEALTH	✛	✛	✛	✛
LUCK	♄			

THURSDAY, 1ST OCTOBER
Sun trine Uranus

The Sun's positive aspect to Uranus will open your eyes to the boundless potential of your career prospects. A whole new avenue of endeavour could

CAPRICORN

unexpectedly come to light, and since this aspect also affects a financial area of your chart, your income could also increase. Benefits are likely to come as the result of modern innovations and technology. A thorough understanding of computing would be advantageous, so make the effort to keep up to date.

FRIDAY, 2ND OCTOBER
Moon opposite Mars

Today you may feel as if you're on a financial roller-coaster. The Moon opposes Mars, so cash doesn't come readily to hand, and when it actually does it's gone all too soon. This may not actually be your fault, as a spendthrift partner might think you are made of money.

SATURDAY, 3RD OCTOBER
Moon square Pluto

Any emotional outbursts today may be down to your insecurities rather than anyone else's behaviour. You could be so irritable that others will feel that they're walking on eggshells when they're around you. If there's a sore subject that you'd rather avoid, then stop drawing attention to it by grumbling. If someone does inadvertently tread on your toes, try not to over-react; you'll only have to apologize later.

SUNDAY, 4TH OCTOBER
Moon conjunct Jupiter

Brothers, sisters, neighbours or colleagues will have interesting news to pass on to you. You may receive an invitation to share a holiday or to go out to an entertaining and interesting event. Someone may even return something that they had borrowed from you, without you having to remind them of it.

MONDAY, 5TH OCTOBER
Venus sextile Pluto

We wouldn't usually class you as a cold, hard schemer, but today you might just prove us wrong! You've got an eye for the main chance and have the power to manipulate others into giving you exactly what you want. Realizing that the direct approach isn't always the right one, your strategies are prepared in advance. This is all well and good, as long as you don't take unfair advantage.

TUESDAY, 6TH OCTOBER
Full Moon

Today's Full Moon puts the spotlight on your career. There have been a lot of changes both externally and within your own mind. Now you have to decide

CAPRICORN

exactly what you want, and in which direction you should proceed. Before you can act you need a plan, so take time to make sure that your strategies for progress are workable. Employers and authority figures will be impressed by your drive and determination.

WEDNESDAY, 7TH OCTOBER
Mars into Virgo

Your desire to overcome injustice and stand up for the rights of others will be best served by expanding your experiences now. Mars moves into your Solar house of education and travel, energizing anything that broadens your personal horizons. There are new challenges to be met, and you'll have little patience with the hypocrisy and double standards you encounter. Knowledge and truth are of prime importance now, and your personal quest to find them starts here.

THURSDAY, 8TH OCTOBER
Moon sextile Jupiter

Your energy levels are on the increase, and you'll feel much more like taking part in life's rich tapestry. There could be interesting news concerning younger members of the family today and if these youngsters are not living with you at the moment, you could pay them a visit now. Whatever you do will be appreciated and you'll be grateful for their efforts on your behalf.

FRIDAY, 9TH OCTOBER
Moon trine Uranus

When you look at your weekly expenses you could be in for something of a nasty shock as you realize how close to the red you actually are. However, this gloomy view won't last as good news is on the way to brighten your outlook. You'll see your situation in a new and more optimistic light.

SATURDAY, 10TH OCTOBER
Mars trine Saturn

You're in the mood for excitement and adventure today, and the chances are that you will be able to indulge yourself to the hilt. You could take part in some kind of competition or enjoy a round of golf, a game of football or a turn on the tennis courts. If your favourite sport is lovemaking, then this could still be your lucky day!

SUNDAY, 11TH OCTOBER
Neptune direct

Neptune goes into direct motion from today which aids your powers of concentration, helping you to put matters into perspective. Any personal

CAPRICORN

impulses that you've concealed for fear of seeming silly or weak-willed can now be admitted. You'll show your innate sensitivity without worrying what others make of your feelings.

MONDAY, 12TH OCTOBER
Mercury into Scorpio

The charitable impulses that make you such an endearing soul could become a liability just now. Mercury moves into your eleventh Solar house, making you a target for every plausible rogue with a story of woe. You are more than prepared to help, but be sure that any cause you support is genuine. At least you're assured of a convivial atmosphere with friends over the next few weeks.

TUESDAY, 13TH OCTOBER
Moon square Mercury

It's a very confusing day on most fronts when your thinking is clouded by the Moon's influence. Red tape, documents, and official correspondence will leave you paralysed with indecision. All you want to do is escape and possibly ask a friend to help out, but friends are as confused as you are. This is not a good time to deal with far-reaching business or financial affairs anyway, so try to leave this for a better occasion.

WEDNESDAY, 14TH OCTOBER
Mercury sextile Mars

A friend's suggestion of a holiday or a short break away from routine should be seriously considered today. You know that the change would do you good, so what's holding you back? Put those ambitions on hold for now and have a break!

THURSDAY, 15TH OCTOBER
Moon trine Saturn

This is a good day for indulging your passions. Any romantic interest or pet hobby will do well, as your attention is directed to expressing your talents. Any ideas you have will now become more real, as you realize their great potential. This marvellous blend of creativity and sound common sense is a winner.

FRIDAY, 16TH OCTOBER
Moon square Pluto

There's no point in taking anything at face value today, unless you want to be conned or confused! You really need to keep your wits about you and carefully analyse any information that comes your way. If you're thinking of travel then take care, for as we all know attractive brochures can be misleading.

CAPRICORN

SATURDAY, 17TH OCTOBER
Mercury square Uranus

You could be pretty weak-willed today, especially if a friend suggests an expensive outing. Not only will you agree immediately, but you'll be inclined to foot the bill as well, no matter how poor your cash flow. Try to be more sensible with money!

SUNDAY, 18TH OCTOBER
Uranus direct

Following Neptune's lead, the erratic planet Uranus also turns direct and could show you new, previously unthought-of sources of income. Unconventional thinking on the subject of money will pay dividends in the future. Don't put too much trust in the tried and true; a more speculative approach may be more beneficial.

MONDAY, 19TH OCTOBER
Mars square Pluto

We're afraid that any stressful aspect between Mars and Pluto tends to put your nerves on edge. It isn't entirely your fault if you're irritable now, since this is a powerful influence and you aren't the only one to feel its malign effects. You have a yearning for freedom at the moment, and this may take the form of needing to escape for a holiday or just to be left alone. Unfortunately, no one seems willing to give you the space you need. Tempers are bound to fray!

TUESDAY, 20TH OCTOBER
New Moon

Your career gets a kick start from the New Moon entering the area of your chart concerned with aspirations, ambition and progress. For many this heralds the start of a new job, for others a chance to branch out on your own. Good luck!

WEDNESDAY, 21ST OCTOBER
Moon square Uranus

You would like a day off! No such luck, we're afraid, for the tense aspect between the Moon and Uranus could certainly disrupt your peace of mind. It could be that you are carrying far too many work worries home, or the burden of an elderly relative is proving too pressing to give you any peace. Fretting won't help, so try to approach problems in a calmer frame of mind.

THURSDAY, 22ND OCTOBER
Sun square Neptune

The stars are not doing much today, so if you can make this a day of rest you'll be doing yourself a favour. You could spend time looking at travel brochures and choosing somewhere nice to go later in the year, or you may enjoy reading or studying. If these ideas don't appeal, just rest.

FRIDAY, 23RD OCTOBER
Sun into Scorpio

The Sun's progress into your Solar area of hopes, wishes and ideals shows that the ball's in your court now. You have all the facts and figures at your disposal, you've thought your prospects through and now it's up to you to make your desires come true. There are risks we admit, but if you really want something then make some positive moves towards attaining it. Good friends will be of enormous help at this time. Be independent and self-motivated and you'll receive all the backing you need, just have courage in your convictions. Venus too lends a helping hand, ensuring that luck is on your side.

SATURDAY, 24TH OCTOBER
Venus into Scorpio

Venus, the planet of harmony, enters your Solar area of friendships from today sparking a period of social activities, fun and new encounters. Romance and social life mingle now, so at the very least this will be a month of flirtation. An old friend may also been seen in a new and more intimate light. If you have any artistic aspirations, you should follow your instincts because the influence of Venus boosts flair and originality.

SUNDAY, 25TH OCTOBER
Saturn into Pisces retrograde

Saturn returns to your house of mental activity today, so you may be faced with a sobering thought that stops you in your tracks. Equally, travel affairs should be put on hold for a while, or at least checked over with a fine-tooth comb!

MONDAY, 26TH OCTOBER
Sun conjunct Venus

You're in a far more influential position than you realize. The conjunction of the Sun and Venus ensures that you present the most pleasing side of your personality. Charm oozes from every pore and your smile is to die for! If you've any professional or personal favours to ask, this is the day for it! Your charisma makes refusal impossible.

CAPRICORN

TUESDAY, 27TH OCTOBER
Moon sextile Mercury

Troubles at work seem to be easing and it may be a female colleague or boss who is helping you out. Your health is improving and you should begin to feel less tired. You could also hear some interesting and amusing news or gossip from a strange or unusual source today.

WEDNESDAY, 28TH OCTOBER
Moon square Sun

A world-weary mood takes a hold under a harsh Lunar aspect to the Sun today. You've endured a lot of pressure recently, and even though the more general outlook is good you are showing the strain. The expectations of others is a major part of the problem. You've done a lot for others recently, but you could honestly do with a day off.

THURSDAY, 29TH OCTOBER
Saturn square Neptune

The vague feeling that 'There's got to be something more to life than this' is the feature of the day. The combined influence of Saturn and Neptune tends to promote unease, and this will affect how you feel. Don't allow this disquiet to descend into despondency.

FRIDAY, 30TH OCTOBER
Moon sextile Saturn

The trouble with you is that you're dutiful to a fault, and put the rest of us to shame. There's little you can't tackle today, since your sharp perception ensures you miss nothing and leave nothing to chance. If others think that you're being pedantic, they're entitled to their opinion. Console yourself with the fable of the ant and the grasshopper: like the ant, you know where your bread is buttered.

SATURDAY, 31ST OCTOBER
Moon conjunct Jupiter

A day of jollity and luck is forecast as the Moon and Jupiter rejoin in one of the most secure areas of your horoscope. You'll have cause to give yourself a pat on the back for a job well done today, and material matters take a turn for the better.

CAPRICORN

November at a Glance

LOVE	♥	♥	
WORK	★		
MONEY	£	£	£
HEALTH	✚		
LUCK	♘	♘	

SUNDAY, 1ST NOVEMBER
Mercury into Sagittarius

Mercury enters the quietest area of your Solar horoscope today, and therefore you cannot expect much to happen in the way of business matters over the next couple of weeks. You may not feel much like talking and you'll probably want to be alone more than is usual. You may be spending time at home because you're feeling off-colour or because you need time to yourself.

MONDAY, 2ND NOVEMBER
Void Moon

There are no important planetary aspects today and even the Moon is unaspected. This kind of a day is called a 'void of course Moon' day, because the Moon is void of aspects during this part of its course. The best way to approach such a day is to do what is normal and natural for you without starting anything new or particularly special.

TUESDAY, 3RD NOVEMBER
Moon square Neptune

You won't know whether you're coming or going today, since the Lunar aspect to Neptune makes it difficult to think straight. It's probably the fault of your family, who won't give you the space you need to work things out in your own way. A lack of suggestions is often a problem, but when there are too many voices it's a nightmare! Try to hide yourself away somewhere or you'll end up irritated and ready for a showdown.

CAPRICORN

WEDNESDAY, 4TH NOVEMBER
Full Moon

An emotional problem seems to be surfacing now which requires a practical solution. You may find that one of your children suddenly becomes unmanageable! You will need to investigate this before working out the best way to tackle the problem. A lover could suddenly spring an unexpected outburst on you, too.

THURSDAY, 5TH NOVEMBER
Moon trine Neptune

You're inspired under the light of Neptune and the Moon today. Creative ventures will give you a sense of accomplishment and prove once and for all that you are unique! You need to relax by doing something that is totally different from your usual duties, such as painting or music. The romantically inclined should have no complaints, because the stars make you receptive to proposals.

FRIDAY, 6TH NOVEMBER
Mercury conjunct Pluto

The outlook today is very deep indeed as you delve into your subconscious in search of your true motivations and views. You may suspect that there's some aspect of your recent actions which has its roots in the distant past, and you'll hunt through your memories until you've found out what it is.

SATURDAY, 7TH NOVEMBER
Mars opposite Jupiter

Take care while travelling today. If you can avoid making any kind of journey now you'll be doing yourself a favour. However, if you must travel, then allow extra time for delays, breakdowns and other frustrations.

SUNDAY, 8TH NOVEMBER
Venus trine Jupiter

Friends will come up with some excellent ideas today, and your luck is in! It may be worth making a small wager or asking someone who owes you money to repay it. If you've been neglecting your pals, then give them a ring and catch up with all their news. If you need practical support, ask a friend to help you.

MONDAY, 9TH NOVEMBER
Venus sextile Mars

A friend may suggest that you join them on an interesting expedition. This does not have to be a trip up the Orinoco river, but maybe a local outing to see something interesting and a little different. You'll enjoy the experience.

CAPRICORN

TUESDAY, 10TH NOVEMBER
Sun trine Jupiter

Monday's influence continues today as a letter or a phone call to a friend may be just the thing to perk you up, especially if you have been feeling rather isolated. There may be some rather good news on the way now, bringing pleasant surprises and unexpected invitations.

WEDNESDAY, 11TH NOVEMBER
Moon square Venus

We know you like to please, but you can take this too far, especially if someone you want to befriend is unresponsive or seems to take your attention for granted. You usually know that goodwill can't be bought, so why are you taking so much trouble to win their approval? Be aware that someone around you is trying to take advantage of your good nature.

THURSDAY, 12TH NOVEMBER
Moon square Pluto

You seem to be the butt of everyone's irrational behaviour at the moment, and your capacity for patience is severely stretched. There's obviously some major drama going on, or possibly it's an over-reaction to a minor matter that has been blown out of all proportion. Our advice is not to rise to the bait, or you'll just be adding fuel to the emotional fire.

FRIDAY, 13TH NOVEMBER
Jupiter direct

Jupiter turns to direct motion today in your third house of communications, and this will bring to an end a period of frustration that has been active for several weeks. It will be easier to contact people that you really do want to see, and there should be little or no difficulty in getting awkward jobs done, especially those that depend upon calling someone in to mend an appliance.

SATURDAY, 14TH NOVEMBER
Sun sextile Mars

With the Sun aspecting Mars in a favourable way leisure and pleasure activities should go well now, especially if an educational element is involved. It may be worth taking a trip to the local library or museum today.

SUNDAY, 15TH NOVEMBER
Moon sextile Mercury

This is the sort of day when your famous subtlety comes into its own. A sensitive

CAPRICORN

approach to work-related issues will be far more productive than any forced solutions. If there are undercurrents in your place of work, a few tactful questions will help you complete a truer picture. However, keep quiet about your ambitions because you could outwit possible rivals.

MONDAY, 16TH NOVEMBER
Moon opposite Saturn

You could be finding it hard to cope with all the pressure around you at the moment. You may want to spend more time with your family just when your job becomes more demanding. Try to balance all the elements as best you can.

TUESDAY, 17TH NOVEMBER
Venus into Sagittarius

Venus moves into your Solar twelfth house today, bringing a period of reflection and retreat. You may not want to do much socializing over the next month or indeed do anything energetic. You seem to want your own company or, perhaps, the company of one trusted friend. Oddly enough, romantic matters and even out-and-out love affairs will prosper now, as long as you keep them quiet for the time being.

WEDNESDAY, 18TH NOVEMBER
Moon trine Jupiter

Happy days are here again as the Moon makes a splendid aspect to fortunate Jupiter. A party atmosphere prevails and there's lots of fun to be had in the company of friends and family.

THURSDAY, 19TH NOVEMBER
New Moon

It's time to show the world what you're made of! The New Moon gives you the chance to show that you've got the initiative and determination to push a project through to a successful conclusion. Anything that requires personal flair combined with the co-operation of colleagues will go well. Don't be afraid to make your mark; you can do anything you set your mind to, so believe in yourself.

FRIDAY, 20TH NOVEMBER
Mercury square Jupiter

You need a holiday, you really do! However, your chances of having one just now are about the same as seeing fat pink piggies flying across the sky! Turn the television to a travel programme and simply dream that you are on that tropical beach, or that the lovely young thing who is strolling along the boulevard is you.

CAPRICORN

SATURDAY, 21ST NOVEMBER
Mercury retrograde

As Mercury goes into backward motion a cloud descends over your thought processes. This influence promotes forgetfulness, wishful thinking and confused communications. Talking at cross purposes and forgetting what you were going to say next are recurrent factors over the next few weeks. Keep writing notes to yourself and you should get through this mixed-up period!

SUNDAY, 22ND NOVEMBER
Sun into Sagittarius

The movement of the Sun into your Solar twelfth house suggests that the next month will be rather quiet and lonely. You may be quite busy on a day-to-day basis, but behind this lies a need to retreat and reflect upon your progress. This is a wonderful time to repay anything that you owe to others, in the form of money and goods or obligations of any kind.

MONDAY, 23RD NOVEMBER
Venus conjunct Pluto

You could fall deeply and madly in love today – with the wrong person! You may be attracted to someone who is mad, bad and dangerous to know. Hopefully you're only dreaming about a television celebrity or pop star, or some other distant personality whom you are unlikely to meet.

TUESDAY, 24TH NOVEMBER
Moon sextile Sun

A mystery will be resolved today and something that you thought you had lost will suddenly turn up. If you have misunderstood someone else's motives, you will now be able to see the reason for their strange behaviour.

WEDNESDAY, 25TH NOVEMBER
Venus sextile Uranus

A woman friend could phone you and suggest an unexpected or last-minute outing. Take her up on her offer because it will be fun, and a money-making scheme may come out of it.

THURSDAY, 26TH NOVEMBER
Moon sextile Saturn

Sometimes it's just not enough to please yourself, so you'll have to take your family into account today, even if it means spending some money. Home improvements are a likely topic now as a partner or relative expounds a plan to

CAPRICORN

transform your home. It may not be in line with your way of thinking, but give it time; you could get to like the idea! You've got to admit that it's practical.

FRIDAY, 27TH NOVEMBER
Neptune into Aquarius

After many years, the misty planet Neptune finally dips its toe into Aquarius – testing the water, one might say! This will profoundly affect your financial fortunes over the next couple of years, and may lead you to more spiritual rather than material goals.

SATURDAY, 28TH NOVEMBER
Mars trine Neptune

'Man does not live by bread alone': that's the motto for you today as you realize that you've got your life under control and it's time to look at deeper values that are every bit as important as practicalities. Matters of conscience are important now, so you should do something about an issue that you feel strongly about. You may be concerned about green issues, homelessness or the plight of the Third World. Remember, you can do something constructive.

SUNDAY, 29TH NOVEMBER
Sun conjunct Pluto

You are in the process of transforming your life in some important way now, and a good deal of this includes a change in your views. However, guard against cutting your nose off to spite your face and downgrading everything that you have achieved so far.

MONDAY, 30TH NOVEMBER
Moon conjunct Saturn

If there's the slightest thing wrong in your home, you'll react like a drill sergeant-major, bawling out the offender and getting your family to toe the line. The combined influence of the Moon and Saturn make you a stickler for detail and no stranger to hard work. There may be a motive in all this attention to cleanliness and good order. Perhaps the visit of an elderly relative is imminent?

CAPRICORN

December at a Glance

LOVE	♥	♥	♥	♥
WORK	★	★		
MONEY	£	£	£	
HEALTH	✛	✛	✛	
LUCK	♘	♘	♘	

TUESDAY, 1ST DECEMBER
Mercury sextile Uranus

You're due for a revelation today, and this unexpected information will benefit your financial fortunes if, and only if, you are swift to act! This bolt from the blue could present you with a bargain that you'd be a fool to pass up.

WEDNESDAY, 2ND DECEMBER
Sun sextile Uranus

Any Solar contact with Uranus is bound to bring a few surprises in its wake. Today is no exception, so follow your instincts where money is concerned, even if they lead you away from the straight and narrow. You'll profit in the end as long as you aren't side-tracked by the more conventional views of friends and colleagues. You know best at the moment, and it's up to you what you do with your cash.

THURSDAY, 3RD DECEMBER
Full Moon

Today's Full Moon is a heavenly signal to think carefully about your working life and day-to-day habits. If you aren't happy then you'd better make up your mind to change things for the better; no one else is going to do it for you. Of course, some opposition is to be expected from those who rather like the *status quo*, but you mustn't allow anyone else's opinions to sway you from a balanced judgement. If you are unemployed, you can be sure that your fortunes will change very soon.

FRIDAY, 4TH DECEMBER
Moon opposite Venus

Don't be tempted along the primrose path of illicit excitement if you can possibly help it! The Lunar opposition to Venus shows that your resistance is likely to be

CAPRICORN

low and you'll be prey to any smooth-talking devil who comes your way! Be strong and turn away such blandishments – but who do we think we're kidding?

SATURDAY, 5TH DECEMBER
Mercury sextile Mars

You may put yourself out to help others today, especially parents or working colleagues. They will appreciate your efforts on their behalf and you will feel good about yourself. You could also have some wild fantasies about where you would like your life to lead. It does no harm to use your imagination sometimes; it will steer you to the right path, if indirectly.

SUNDAY, 6TH DECEMBER
Moon trine Jupiter

If you are offered an opportunity to work in partnership with someone else, then do consider this today. The work that is involved may be some kind of business, but it could be a fund-raising project or helping with a local event. There is a sporty feeling to the day, so take time to enjoy sporting activities.

MONDAY, 7TH DECEMBER
Moon sextile Mars

The Moon makes a good aspect to Mars today, so for those of you who are working the career picture looks more promising. This is not a time to ignore material affairs such as pension plans, insurance policies and all sorts of shared resources. A little attention paid to your long-term security will pay ample dividends.

TUESDAY, 8TH DECEMBER
Moon trine Sun

Today your confidence will be on a real high and you will be absolutely sure that you're right. A romance or relationship will begin to improve now and you'll have a real chance to resolve any misunderstandings that have arisen between you. You will be able to explain how you feel to your lover, and you will have an almost psychic understanding of his or her needs.

WEDNESDAY, 9TH DECEMBER
Venus trine Saturn

A harmonious day is forecast for your family and home. If there has been any tension you'll reach a renewed understanding as everyone lays their cards on the table. You'll find that differences aren't as divisive as you may have feared.

CAPRICORN

THURSDAY, 10TH DECEMBER
Moon square Sun

Some days are far easier than others, as we're sure you've found recently. You're in a cycle of urgent activity one day and total exhaustion the next. This is an 'exhausted day'; you really can't get motivated about duties or pressing family engagements, so do yourself a favour and think up a good excuse to get time off.

FRIDAY, 11TH DECEMBER
Venus into Capricorn

There's an upsurge in optimism today as Venus, planet of love, enters your own sign. This should put a much needed sparkle back into your life and you'll find your popularity increases in the coming weeks. You can't fail to charm all around you, for who could resist your smouldering looks and magnetic attraction? Charisma is your middle name from now on, so make the most of it.

SATURDAY, 12TH DECEMBER
Mars sextile Pluto

With Mars aspecting Pluto today you'll be very capable and ambitious. Although you are busy, your mind will be working overtime devising far-reaching professional strategies.

SUNDAY, 13TH DECEMBER
Moon sextile Sun

Stop and reflect upon what you have achieved. You deserve a reward for all your hard work, so treat yourself to something nice. A sense of self-satisfaction is evident today, and it's totally justified. Well done!

MONDAY, 14TH DECEMBER
Moon sextile Venus

You're back to being one of the most sentimental people around. The Moon aspects Venus now, which makes you as weak as water and easily persuaded that black was white. You're so susceptible to emotional arguments that it'll be unwise to part with any cash. Your inclinations lead you to more gentle, possibly romantic pastimes, so forget worldly issues and concentrate on fun for today.

TUESDAY, 15TH DECEMBER
Mars trine Uranus

With Mars forming a very favourable aspect with Uranus, a surprise windfall is on the cards for many today. A hint from a man could set you on a new and quite unexpected professional course, which will bring profit in its wake.

CAPRICORN

WEDNESDAY, 16TH DECEMBER
Moon sextile Neptune

It's important to relax today. The pressures of the working world have taken their toll, and you need to indulge yourself in the personal realm of your imagination. A good television programme or film will take you out of yourself, and if you can share the experience with a close friend, it will be even more fulfilling.

THURSDAY, 17TH DECEMBER
Moon sextile Uranus

You need something exciting to happen just to make you feel worthwhile – and that's exactly what's on offer today. The Moon makes a good aspect to Uranus, turning your attention to the finer things in life. A shopping trip will yield a surprising bargain, perhaps something tastefully artistic for your home.

FRIDAY, 18TH DECEMBER
New Moon

A New Moon in the most psychic area of your chart suggests that the next month will bring you closer to intuitive, psychic and spiritual matters than ever before. You may have prophetic dreams or strange feelings that seem to portend future events. Areas of life that you have never before explored may suddenly become important.

SATURDAY, 19TH DECEMBER
Sun trine Saturn

With the Sun in the Solar house of reflection, some time spent alone at home thinking about old times will put all your present concerns into perspective. A period of solitude and relaxation will be just what you need to cope with the pressures of life.

SUNDAY, 20TH DECEMBER
Moon square Mars

Stress is something we all have to deal with now and again, but when it reaches the stage where you are so irritable that people go out of their way to avoid you, then it's time to take action. Try some deep-breathing exercises or take up meditation. You can't do much about outside events, but you can influence your reactions.

MONDAY, 21ST DECEMBER
Mercury conjunct Pluto

There is so much going on behind the scenes in your life that it's impossible to keep track of it all. You seem destined to make some kind of important transformation in your life, and you are in the planning stages of this now.

CAPRICORN

TUESDAY, 22ND DECEMBER
Sun into Capricorn

The Sun moves into your own sign today, highlighting your image and increasing your self-confidence. It's all a matter of accentuating the positive and eliminating the negative.

WEDNESDAY, 23RD DECEMBER
Mercury sextile Uranus

Your brain is working overtime today. Mercury makes a good aspect to Uranus, giving you a wealth of innovative, original ideas. The trouble is that they're coming at such a fast and furious pace that you forget many along the way. Keep a notebook handy to jot down your inspirations, because it would be a crying shame to lose the least of them.

THURSDAY, 24TH DECEMBER
Moon square Pluto

For once tactlessness isn't a fault, because the Lunar aspect to Pluto ensures that straight talking is far more important than mere politeness. Your opinion will be asked, and a candid reply will be appreciated. For once you can be truthful without fear of the consequences, even if the subject under discussion is extremely controversial.

FRIDAY, 25TH DECEMBER
Moon conjunct Jupiter

The phone will bring some kind of unexpected opportunity your way today. This may be an opportunity to join your friends and neighbours for a Christmas celebration, and there may also be fortunate news from brothers and sisters. Have a happy Christmas Day.

SATURDAY, 26TH DECEMBER
Moon square Sun

It's a difficult day emotionally, simply because you feel a sense of unease that's hard to pin down. The outlook isn't improved by the harsh Lunar aspect to the Sun, which sets your nerves on edge and gives a restlessness that's hard for you, or indeed anyone, else to live with. After the festivities you may feel you need some space, so get out and about. Relatives, especially older females, may irritate you by not crediting your intelligence.

CAPRICORN

SUNDAY, 27TH DECEMBER
Moon square Venus

It's one of those days when things get on top of you. Even treasured possessions may come to represent regrets or frustrations. Your outlook is gloomy, but console yourself with the thought that this too shall pass. The security you have built for you and your family will stand the test of time.

MONDAY, 28TH DECEMBER
Mercury sextile Mars

What you are thinking and what you are saying are two different things today. You may say what others want to hear, or you may simply try to keep the peace, but your inner thoughts may be much more turbulent than others realize. Your mind is pin-sharp now and your intellect's verging on genius level!

TUESDAY, 29TH DECEMBER
Saturn direct

Saturn turns to direct motion now, and this should bring an end to any delays and muddles in connection with property or premises. If you want to move house or raise money for a mortgage, this should be much easier from now on.

WEDNESDAY, 30TH DECEMBER
Moon trine Neptune

The Moon aspects Neptune today, making you prone to odd fears and a generalized sort of anxiety. Fortunately, help is at hand! We know you aren't a fan of advice, but you'd do well to listen to some well thought-out words from a colleague.

THURSDAY, 31ST DECEMBER
Moon trine Mars

A healthy body and a healthy mind will ensure your success now. The mixed rays of the Moon and Mars make you conscious of both your physique and the need to maintain a positive mental attitude. Self-confidence is vital now as you can increase your prestige in a career situation by pushing yourself forward. If you've been troubled by nagging ailments, then have them checked out to set your mind at rest. Begin the new year with a happy healthy you!

CAPRICORN

1999

January at a Glance

LOVE	♥				
WORK	★	★	★	★	★
MONEY	£	£	£	£	£
HEALTH	☉	☉	☉	☉	
LUCK	♘	♘	♘	♘	♘

FRIDAY, 1ST JANUARY
Mercury square Jupiter

You need a holiday, you really do. However, your chances of having one as the new year begins are about the same as seeing a flock of fat pink piggies strolling across the sky! Turn the television to a travel programme and simply dream that you are on that tropical beach or the lovely young thing who is strolling along the boulevard is you.

SATURDAY, 2ND JANUARY
Full Moon

The Full Moon shines in the area of close relationships today. Since it is a stress indicator, you'd be wise to build some bridges within a close partnership, either that or be content to let an emotional link drift, possibly away! Your understanding and tolerance will be the key to relationship success.

SUNDAY, 3RD JANUARY
Moon opposite Venus

Your loved ones may be in a techy mood today, so steer clear of domestic disputes and try to get your lover and the kids to relax. Snuggle up in front of the fire, toast a few crumpets and open a bottle of something nice and warming. Get a pack of cards out or try your hand at a bit of Scrabble. This way, you will keep the domestic harmony going whilst avoiding getting cold and wet at the same time!

CAPRICORN

MONDAY, 4TH JANUARY
Venus into Aquarius

Your financial state should experience a welcome boost for a few weeks as Venus, one of the planetary indicators of wealth, today moves into your Solar house of possessions and economic security. You feel that you deserve a lifestyle full of luxury and that will be reflected in the good taste you express when making purchases for your home. Your sense of self-worth is boosted too, which might indicate a renewed interest in high fashion.

TUESDAY, 5TH JANUARY
Venus conjunct Neptune

There is a highly artistic and creative feel to the day as Venus meets Neptune. This shows that there's money to be made from the exercise of your gifts. Those involved in the fashion industry, the arts or entertainment will benefit from an increase in income. In fact, anyone who uses flair and originality in their job will do well. The conjunction of these sensitive planets also directs you to dealing with jewellery or glassware. You may find that you posess a valuable antique.

WEDNESDAY, 6TH JANUARY
Moon square Pluto

You seem to be the butt of everyone's irrational behaviour at the moment and your capacity for patience is severely stretched. There's obviously some major drama going on, or possibly it's an over-reaction to a minor matter which has been blown out of all proportion. Don't rise to the bait or you'll be adding fuel to the emotional fire.

THURSDAY, 7TH JANUARY
Mercury into Capricorn

The movement of Mercury into your own sign signals the start of a period of much clearer thinking for you. You will know where you want to go and what you want to do from now on. It will be quite easy for you to influence others with the brilliance of your ideas and you will be able to project just the right image. Guard against trying to crowd too much into one day.

FRIDAY, 8TH JANUARY
Moon trine Venus

Attend to practical matters today and deal with anything to do with money. If you talk to your bank manager about finances for a business idea, you will get some really useful advice and all the help you require to go along with this. If you need to save up for some kind of future event or project, then set this in motion soon.

CAPRICORN

SATURDAY, 9TH JANUARY
Moon square Sun

There could be some kind of power struggle going on today. In practical terms, this could bring you up against an authority figure or someone who thinks rather a lot of themselves. This could also make things difficult for any business dealings that you have on the go at the moment. However, on a less practical note, you may doubt your own judgement for a while.

SUNDAY, 10TH JANUARY
Moon opposite Saturn

Sometimes you feel hemmed in and far too restricted in your actions by those who don't understand your motivations or good qualities. You don't like miserable people at the best of times since you find that the mood seems to rub off. Unfortunately, it's just one of those days when you encounter grim folk again and again. Keep smiling and don't take their negativity to heart.

MONDAY, 11TH JANUARY
Moon square Uranus

The Moon makes a square aspect to Uranus today so anything, literally anything, can be expected from your friends now. You'll be encouraged to throw caution to the winds and indulge yourself in carefree pleasures. The only problem is that some people around you are equally free with your money. Keep a close watch on those who don't seem to be paying their way. Make sure that you aren't being taken for a ride.

TUESDAY, 12TH JANUARY
Venus sextile Pluto

There is a terrible temptation to push the financial boat out too far today. Venus's self-indulgent angle to Pluto prompts you to spend more than you can afford on luxuries and pleasure. You deserve a little treat now and again, but when the treat expands out of all measure to your income, it's time to call a halt. Try to keep the flow of cash within reasonable bounds.

WEDNESDAY, 13TH JANUARY
Venus conjunct Uranus

You are rather bored with routine and tired of doing only those things that are expected of you. Today's conjunction of Venus and Uranus brings your rebellious tendencies to the fore. In a financial sense, this is not good news, since you're gripped by a spending fever. Mind you, this is an expensive time of year anyway, so extra spending shouldn't be too much of a shock to the system. Don't be afraid

CAPRICORN

to be yourself. Experiment with any new concept or activity that takes your fancy. You need some excitement in your life.

THURSDAY, 14TH JANUARY
Sun sextile Jupiter

A pleasant surprise could come winging your way through the post today. There may be an invitation to visit far-distant friends or relatives, or a holiday offer advertised in a brochure or in the newspapers that you really shouldn't miss. New neighbours or colleagues will turn out to be pleasant and amiable and you could start a new friendship or make useful new contacts.

FRIDAY, 15TH JANUARY
Sun square Mars

You will feel that you are right but others could be just as attached to their own point of view. You are entitled to your opinion but it would be a good idea to use a little tact and diplomacy, especially if you feel the need to disagree with your superiors at work today.

SATURDAY, 16TH JANUARY
Moon conjunct Mercury

You are likely to be the starring act today wherever you happen to be. At work, your ideas will beam out far ahead of those of others, and at home your scintillating wit will impress your family and friends. You will be so sharp that you are in danger of cutting yourself on your own tongue!

SUNDAY, 17TH JANUARY
New Moon

There is a New Moon in your own sign. This is a powerfully positive influence that encourages you to make a new start. Personal opportunities are about to change your life. You must now be prepared to leave the past behind to embark on a brand new course. Decide what you want, because you'll be your own best guide.

MONDAY, 18TH JANUARY
Sun square Saturn

In family affairs, it is too easy to take a negative, defeatist view at the moment. You're looking on the black side, blowing all problems out of proportion. Financial worries may loom large but they aren't as drastic as you seem to think. Family members are a cause of worry but many of your anxieties are needless. Be realistic, and that means weigh the good with the bad, and not only look at one side of the coin.

CAPRICORN

TUESDAY, 19TH JANUARY
Moon conjunct Venus

If you are feeling at all weak, then don't venture anywhere near expensive shops because you're too prone to the impulse-buying syndrome today. Attractiveness is more important to you than value at the moment, so the temptation to blow your cash on a luxury item is too strong for comfort. Hoard your resources and leave shopping trips until you're less impetuous.

WEDNESDAY, 20TH JANUARY
Sun into Aquarius

Your financial prospects take an upturn from today as the Sun enters your house of money and possessions. The next month should see an improvement in your economic security. It may be that you need to lay plans to ensure maximum profit. Don't expect any swift returns from investments but lay down a pattern for future growth. Sensible monetary decisions made now will pay off in a big way.

THURSDAY, 21ST JANUARY
Mars opposite Saturn

Your patience could be sorely stretched today because everyone around you is very demanding. Both at work and in the domestic area, people want you to be in two places at once, doing at least three things and probably juggling as well! Try to keep a rein on your temper!

FRIDAY, 22ND JANUARY
Sun conjunct Neptune

As the Sun meets up with Neptune you could now be far too sensitive for your own good. You are prone to making problems where none exists. Emotionally, you'll be rather vulnerable, too ready to take idle comments as barbed insults. Keep away from money dealings and far-reaching business decisions or you'll regret them when it is too late to turn back. On the other hand, artistic or theatrical interests will do well.

SATURDAY, 23RD JANUARY
Mercury sextile Jupiter

You seem to have grown a wonderful business head on your shoulders almost overnight. Your thinking will have an icy clarity today and your perception will be as sharp as a knife. You will see just where to make the best deal for yourself and you will be able to work out just which path your adversaries are unsuccessfully trying to lead you down. A fascinating day.

CAPRICORN

SUNDAY, 24TH JANUARY
Mercury square Saturn

No matter what you intend to say to your family today, the message is bound to be garbled or come out harsher and more autocratic than you intend. You have everyone's best interests at heart, but it might be better to leave an important announcement until you can choose your words with more care. We wouldn't want to needlessly offend anyone, would we?

MONDAY, 25TH JANUARY
Moon square Uranus

Beware of thinly disguised excuses for overspending today. A child, or at least someone younger than yourself, has been dipping into the reserves as if money was going out of fashion and now expects you to bail them out. The cunning involved in this exercise, to make you feel responsible or even guilty, for someone else's self-indulgence is remarkable. However, it does give you a difficult choice. Do you open your purse or do you leave them to it to teach them a lesson?

TUESDAY, 26TH JANUARY
Mars into Scorpio

Friends are likely to be a strong influence on you at this time. Old friends may have interesting ideas to put your way, while new ones could come crowding into your life quite quickly. You may join some kind of very active group who share your interests and are keen to have you as part of their organization. This may have something to do with sports or some other kind of energetic or outdoor activity.

WEDNESDAY, 27TH JANUARY
Venus sextile Saturn

Though domestic circumstances are a drain on your bank account, the happy influence of Venus lifts your spirits and provides just a little extra cash to ease your burden.

THURSDAY, 28TH JANUARY
Venus into Pisces

If you've got any favours to ask, the passage of Venus into your Solar house of persuasion shows that you can use considerable charm and eloquence to win others over to your viewpoint. A little flirtation combined with a winning way ensures that you achieve your desires. Your creative talents are boosted too, so perhaps you should consider writing down your inspirations.

CAPRICORN

FRIDAY, 29TH JANUARY
Venus trine Mars

A friend may declare feelings of love for you today, or conversely, you may find yourself being extremely attracted to a friend or an acquaintance. Love could come your way as a result of joining in some kind of group activity. Even if things are not as exciting as this, good friendships can be formed and loyal and loving companions can be found.

SATURDAY, 30TH JANUARY
Sun sextile Pluto

There could be some very interesting news today that will have a favourable effect on your financial situation. People or organizations that you are attached to seem to be doing quite well, and this will have the effect of improving your chances of earning more money or of gaining promotion.

SUNDAY, 31ST JANUARY
Full Moon eclipse

There is an eclipse of the Moon today which will affect two areas of your life in a rather profound way. Firstly, it may be that your job is going through a patch of turbulence and this may even bring you close to making a change of some kind. It may be worth waiting until the dust has settled a bit before making any sweeping changes. Your health may let you down now too. If so, don't leave things to chance.

February at a Glance

LOVE	♥	♥	
WORK	★	★	
MONEY	£	£	£
HEALTH	✛	✛	✛
LUCK	♘	♘	

MONDAY, 1ST FEBRUARY
Mars square Neptune

Something you've wanted for a long time comes into reach today, but is it really

CAPRICORN

worth having? If it is a particular item, is the price too high, or its true value too low? Think before you purchase today!

TUESDAY, 2ND FEBRUARY
Sun conjunct Uranus

Anything can happen and probably will as the Sun conjuncts Uranus in your Solar house of possessions and finance. Nothing will go to plan, but that may not be a bad thing. You may get a windfall today, but, on the other hand, you tend to be so careless with your cash that it will be gone before the money has had a chance to settle in. Be as flexible as you can and try not to make any firm arrangements.

WEDNESDAY, 3RD FEBRUARY
Sun conjunct Mercury

This is an excellent day on which to pull off a really spectacular deal, so if you feel like wheeling and dealing in the big leagues, then do so today! Even if you are only looking around for something for yourself or your family, you should be able to find just what you want. This is also the time for buying or selling a vehicle, or for getting one put back into good working order.

THURSDAY, 4TH FEBRUARY
Moon opposite Jupiter

If you feel like becoming the last of the big spenders today, then try to hold your horses. Get someone else to look after your credit cards and your cheque book because you simply won't be able to restrain yourself. Keep away from those tempting pictures in the catalogues and stay out of the shops. Send someone else out to do the weekly food shopping today!

FRIDAY, 5TH FEBRUARY
Mercury conjunct Uranus

Keep a tight grip on the purse strings today for sudden expenses are bound to come up which could leave you short. Mercury conjuncts Uranus which shows that you could be easily persuaded into parting with your cash. Remember that whenever Uranus is activated in your chart, a bolt from the blue swiftly follows. Today it is money, so keep your wits about you.

SATURDAY, 6TH FEBRUARY
Venus square Pluto

You fall prey to some intense emotions today. It is all the fault of Venus and Pluto who conspire to bring some quite disturbing undercurrents to the surface. However, though the initial shock may be uncomfortable, it's not altogether bad,

CAPRICORN

since certain things have to be said and you may as well lay your cards on the table now. This planetary influence indicates a clearing of the air.

SUNDAY, 7TH FEBRUARY
Moon conjunct Mars

Lonely ladies who are reading this have a terrific opportunity of meeting someone new today and it would happen in the most unexpected way. The rest of you can enjoy sporting activities or anything that you do with friends on a group or a social setting. Phone your friends and suggest a game of golf or something similar.

MONDAY, 8TH FEBRUARY
Moon square Sun

You may decide to treat a friend to a meal out or to a small luxury of some kind. This would be a great idea if you could be sure that your friend would appreciate your generosity. Unfortunately, he or she may take this for granted and your efforts will be wasted.

TUESDAY, 9TH FEBRUARY
Moon trine Jupiter

Friends will want to talk over some of their problems today and you will be happy to lend a listening ear. You may feel like off-loading some of your worries on them too and the whole exercise will help you to put things into perspective again. This is also a rather lucky day for money and a gamble may pay off.

WEDNESDAY, 10TH FEBRUARY
Moon sextile Uranus

You need something exciting to happen just to make you feel worthwhile and that is exactly what's on offer today. The Moon makes a good aspect to Uranus, turning your attention to the finer things in life. A shopping trip will yield a surprising bargain, perhaps something tastefully artistic as an ornament to your home, or indeed your person.

THURSDAY, 11TH FEBRUARY
Mercury sextile Saturn

This is a great time to get something that you need for the home. Any goods that you buy now would stand the test of time and be worth the money that you spend on them. An older family member may turn out to be very helpful to you today, especially in connection with family or domestic matters.

CAPRICORN

FRIDAY, 12TH FEBRUARY
Mercury into Pisces

Your mind will be going at full speed ahead over the next few weeks and you are bound to come up with some really great new ideas. You will be very busy with the phone ringing and letters arriving by the ton. You will find yourself acting as a temporary secretary for a while, even if the only person who makes use of your services is yourself.

SATURDAY, 13TH FEBRUARY
Jupiter into Aries

Your innate kindness and compassion for others is being stimulated now by the entry of Jupiter in your Solar area of family, home and heritage. Your protective instincts will be strongly stimulated in the coming months. However, you may tend to be rather possessive, without allowing loved ones the opportunity of standing on their own two feet.

SUNDAY, 14TH FEBRUARY
Moon sextile Jupiter

Moneywise and in dealings with authority, you're in luck on St Valentine's Day. A marvellous astral combination ensures that you won't take less than perfect and are forceful and assertive. Just make sure that you don't take this wilfulness too far, otherwise you could end up dishing out far more than anyone deserves. At least you are going to get what you want.

MONDAY, 15TH FEBRUARY
Moon conjunct Uranus

The Lunar conjunction with Uranus makes your restlessness quite difficult to bear. You want to be off searching for new sensations and experiences, but in most cases the financial situation won't allow you to roam too far afield. You're in no mood to follow established guidelines and practices. You'd far rather set off on a direction of your own.

TUESDAY, 16TH FEBRUARY
New Moon eclipse

There is a New Moon eclipse in your Solar house of personal finances and personal possessions, and this will bring a problem to a head in connection with money, land, property or goods that belong to you. There are many ways that this could affect you but one possibility is that you have some kind of dispute over who owns what.

CAPRICORN

WEDNESDAY, 17TH FEBRUARY
Sun sextile Saturn

Luck seems to be with you at the moment, and even better still, today's excellent aspect between the Sun and Saturn, suggests that any plans that you start to put into operation now will go very well in both the short and the long term.

THURSDAY, 18TH FEBRUARY
Mercury square Pluto

You may have been prone to a nagging worry connected to a health matter. This has gone on long enough and now you should discuss this anxiety with someone who understands the problem.

FRIDAY, 19TH FEBRUARY
Sun into Pisces

Your curiosity will be massively stimulated from today as the Sun enters the area of learning and communication. Other people's business suddenly becomes your own. That's not to say that you turn into a busybody overnight, it's just that many will turn to you for some guidance. Affairs in the lives of your brothers, sisters and neighbours have extra importance. Short journeys are well starred for one month.

SATURDAY, 20TH FEBRUARY
Void Moon

This is one of those days when none of the planets is making any worthwhile kind of aspect to any of the others. Even the Moon is 'void of course', which means that it is not making aspects of any importance to the other planets. On such a day, avoid starting anything new and don't set out to do anything important. Do what needs to be done and take some time off for a rest.

SUNDAY, 21ST FEBRUARY
Venus into Aries

Old scores and family squabbles can now be laid to rest as the passage of Venus into your domestic area signals a time of harmony and contentment. Surround yourself with beauty, both in terms of affection and in material possessions. This is a good time to renew a closeness with those you love. Join forces to complete a major project such as redecoration, or even a move of home itself. Be assured that the stars smile on you.

MONDAY, 22ND FEBRUARY
Venus sextile Neptune

You tend to wear your heart on your sleeve when Venus affectionately aspects

CAPRICORN

Neptune. You're a generous soul and your kindness is self-evident now when you'd go to any lengths to assist those who need your help. It may be that all that is required is a shoulder to cry on, but even if more practical aid is necessary, you'll be unstinting in your generosity.

TUESDAY, 23RD FEBRUARY
Moon opposite Pluto

Paranoia is far too easy a trap to fall into today. The odd word or furtive gesture will get you wondering if you aren't the dupe in some plot or other. Though you may be suspicious, you should not leap to any conclusions too hastily. Wait until you've got some evidence before you confront anyone. In work especially, play it cool.

WEDNESDAY, 24TH FEBRUARY
Venus conjunct Jupiter

There seems to be a wonderful opportunity around for you to repair any bad feeling that has been occurring in or around your family today. You can also set out to buy goods that will make you more comfortable at home. If, for example, you have been on the lookout for a new carpet, a new set of bed linen or anything else that will improve the look and the feel of your home, today is the day that you could find this.

THURSDAY, 25TH FEBRUARY
Moon trine Sun

This is a day to be sociable and outgoing. An invitation received now should be accepted at once, no matter what reservations or prior arrangements you have. A meeting with friends and neighbours could lead to a possible romance. If you're already hitched, take your other half on a magical tour of the social scene. Fun and laughs all round.

FRIDAY, 26TH FEBRUARY
Sun trine Mars

An active social life is on offer today! This is no time to sit moping around the house, get out and enjoy yourself in the company of good friends. Go to a dance or a sporting event. You'll love every minute.

SATURDAY, 27TH FEBRUARY
Jupiter sextile Neptune

The hectic social whirl can go its own way as far as you're concerned as the combination of Jupiter and Neptune puts you into a contemplative frame of mind.

CAPRICORN

You'll be happiest when solitary today, since the peace and quiet will help you to sort out your priorities and count your blessings.

SUNDAY, 28TH FEBRUARY
Moon opposite Uranus

Any Lunar aspect to Uranus has surprising consequences, good and bad. When this influence hits the financial areas of your chart you could be in for something of a shock. Perhaps an unexpected bill has turned up or you haven't taken a large expense into account. Look over your books once more to check that you aren't committing a serious error. Take extra care of the cash flow today.

March at a Glance

LOVE	♥	♥	♥
WORK	★		
MONEY	£	£	£
HEALTH	✚	✚	
LUCK	U	U	U

MONDAY, 1ST MARCH
Saturn into Taurus

You'll feel rather vulnerable today. Saturn is to blame for this outbreak of self-doubt and anxiety. You will definitely need someone understanding around to bolster your flagging self-confidence. Most of your worries seem to centre on money.

TUESDAY, 2ND MARCH
Mercury into Pisces

Your life is going to be extremely busy for a while and there will be little time to sit around and rest. You will have more to do with friends, relatives, colleagues and neighbours than is usual, and you could spend quite a bit of time dealing with minor domestic and work problems with workmen and women of various kinds. You may also spend time and money sorting out a vehicle.

CAPRICORN

WEDNESDAY, 3RD MARCH
Venus trine Pluto

If you feel like a plant that's been stunted in growth and not allowed to follow its natural course, today's stellar influences allow you the chance to throw off burdens of the past and express yourself freely. Hang-ups and complexes will no longer provide a barrier to your progress in emotional affairs. You at last see where you are going and what's best for you.

THURSDAY, 4TH MARCH
Venus sextile Uranus

Expect the unexpected today, because if you had planned to spend a nice quiet day at home, this is not how it is going to be. You could have friends dropping in on you throughout the day, and while you love to have their company, it will make it impossible for you to get on with your housework.

FRIDAY, 5TH MARCH
Mercury sextile Neptune

Renewed understandings are the order of the day as Mercury, planet of communication, aspects the sensitive Neptune. The most delicate matters can now be discussed without anyone being embarrassed or ashamed of past actions and differences. You are on the path to familial harmony now. Perhaps a shared project such as redecoration will inspire some laughs, and everyone needs that!

SATURDAY, 6TH MARCH
Moon square Neptune

An unexpected setback will prevent you from being able to achieve your heart's desire today. You may feel in the mood to pursue your dreams but unfortunately you won't be able to do this for a while yet.

SUNDAY, 7TH MARCH
Moon square Uranus

Don't be taken in by any shady, fly-by-night schemes that a friend with more money than sense tries to promote today. You must keep your feet on the ground and recognize that high-flown plans and big ideas for profit are nothing more than hot air. The packaging may be attractive but you should have the good sense not to fall for a get-rich-quick scheme.

MONDAY, 8TH MARCH
Moon trine Venus

The finer things of life have a delightful appeal today. You're in a cultured frame of

CAPRICORN

mind susceptible to refined music and fine art. There's also a romantic side to this Venusian influence, so it's a time to indulge yourself in pleasure.

TUESDAY, 9TH MARCH
Moon trine Jupiter

Your home and domestic circumstances are really rather good at present, and whatever you have in mind for yourself and your family will go particularly well today. You may be keen to move house or to put an existing home into some kind of order, and it looks as though the opportunity to do this is fast approaching.

WEDNESDAY, 10TH MARCH
Mercury retrograde

Whenever Mercury moves into retrograde motion, life becomes difficult for a while, therefore, over the next few weeks, you can expect to be subject to a number of delays and frustrations. People who owe you money may delay payment, letters could go missing in the post and travel plans will be awkward and muddled. You may find it hard to get on with others and your own nerves may be on edge.

THURSDAY, 11TH MARCH
Moon square Mercury

There will be a number of ups and downs today which will have your emotions swinging from one extreme to another. Someone may say something that really upsets you, and worse still, makes you doubt yourself. If you talk this over with a friend or a relative, you will find that they are just as outraged as you are at the unpleasant way you have been treated. It's nice to find out who your friends are.

FRIDAY, 12TH MARCH
Moon sextile Mars

You have put in more than your fair share of work and worry recently and now is the time to relax with a few friends. Male friends would probably be more fun than female ones at the moment and something like a game of sports with a few manly, muscular pals would be just the thing to put you back into top form. Even if all you can manage is a few words over the garden fence, then go for it today.

SATURDAY, 13TH MARCH
Mercury sextile Neptune

You are likely to be prone to some financial worries that are connected with your home. However, the optimistic planets will show that many of your fears have been groundless. A new allocation of your resources is possible. You may find that you can reduce debts or repayments in some way.

CAPRICORN

SUNDAY, 14TH MARCH
Moon sextile Pluto

A realization about your own self-worth is long overdue, so when Luna and Pluto conspire to make you delve into the depths of your mind you'll find that your dreams can provide a rich source of inspiration. Another aspect of the link between the Moon and Pluto could boost your income from a secret source. Keep the news of this good fortune to yourself.

MONDAY, 15TH MARCH
Moon sextile Venus

A woman will prove to be very helpful to you now. She may help you to sort out a domestic problem and she could suggest ways to save money. If you need to employ someone to help in or around the house, the right person will come to the fore today. There are bargains to be had at the shops, so get out and have a look around while the opportunity is there for you.

TUESDAY, 16TH MARCH
Moon square Pluto

Any emotional outburst made today is likely to be more the result of your own insecurities than any action by someone else. You could be so irritable that others will feel that they're walking on eggshells when they're around you. If there's a sore subject that you'd really like avoided, then stop drawing attention to it by grumbling. If someone does inadvertently tread on your toes, try not to over-react because you'll only have to apologize later.

WEDNESDAY, 17TH MARCH
New Moon

The New Moon shows a change in your way of thinking. In many ways you'll know that it's time to move on. Perhaps you'll find yourself in a new company, a new home or among a new circle of friends in the near future. Opinions are set to change as you are influenced by more stimulating people. Perhaps you'll consider taking up an educational course of some kind.

THURSDAY, 18TH MARCH
Venus into Taurus

This is a good day to begin new projects and to get great ideas off the ground. Venus is now moving into the area of your chart that is concerned with creativity, so over the next few weeks you can take advantage of this and get involved with some kind of creative process. Venus is concerned with the production of beauty, so utilize this planetary energy to enhance any of your creations.

CAPRICORN

FRIDAY, 19TH MARCH
Sun conjunct Mercury

There is no doubt that your mental powers are on top form today. The conjunction of the Sun and Mercury lets your intelligence shine. You are particularly persuasive too, so it shouldn't be difficult to win even the most stubborn and entrenched person over to your cause.

SATURDAY, 20TH MARCH
Venus conjunct Saturn

Love can show itself in many ways. Though one tends to think of hearts and flowers, it is in the qualities of loyalty and devotion that lasting value is found. These fine feelings will stand out today, as a lover or close friend shows how highly you stand in their affections. This may not be one of the most enjoyable days on record but when it comes to trust and depth it cannot be beaten.

SUNDAY, 21ST MARCH
Sun into Aries

The home and family become your main interest over the next four weeks as the Sun moves into the most domestic area of your chart from today. Family feuds will now be resolved, and you'll find an increasing contentment in your own surroundings. A haven of peace will be restored in your home. This should also be a period of nostalgia when happy memories come flooding back.

MONDAY, 22ND MARCH
Moon trine Neptune

The Moon aspects Neptune today making you prone to odd fears and a generalized sort of anxiety. Fortunately, help is at hand. You aren't a fan of advice but you'd do well to listen to some well-considered words from a colleague today. Your worries will probably include money, work and health. In all these areas it is best to find out where you stand to put your mind at rest.

TUESDAY, 23RD MARCH
Venus square Neptune

You definitely need a reality check today! The aspect between Neptune and Venus doesn't make for a sober or practical outlook. In fact, you'd be far more likely to dream your time away accomplishing very little at all. The artistically inclined could experience some sort of creative block that will be hard to shift.

CAPRICORN

WEDNESDAY, 24TH MARCH
Moon square Sun

There may be some tension and conflict in your home today, and you and your lover may find yourselves out of sympathy with each other for a while. One of you may be off-colour (or even pre-menstrual?) and this may be at the back of the afflicted one's tetchy and awkward mood. Family members may undermine your confidence in yourself and in your abilities. All in all, a rather foul day.

THURSDAY, 25TH MARCH
Sun sextile Neptune

You are in an extremely charitable and caring frame of mind today. The Sun makes a good aspect to Neptune, showing your readiness to give your time, money and energy to a worthy cause. Your selflessness is an uplifting influence and your sense of spiritual well-being is enhanced. This aspect also encourages peace, so make an attempt to win over a difficult family member. You can pour oil on troubled waters and resolve old feuds.

FRIDAY, 26TH MARCH
Moon square Saturn

Anxiety is the order of the day. The Moon is in hard aspect to Saturn which makes the slightest extra expense a cause for concern. You may feel that you need a break from the old routine, but no matter how hard you try, you can't seem to make the books balance to allow you to get away. Be calm, the outlook isn't as bad as you think. The monetary situation will soon take a turn for the better.

SATURDAY, 27TH MARCH
Venus opposite Mars

Social groups can be volatile when everyone wants their own way! That's the picture today when reasonable viewpoints and logical arguments come up against very unreasonable people. The opposition between Venus and Mars provides a good case for being solitary just now.

SUNDAY, 28TH MARCH
Void Moon

Occasionally, one finds a day on which neither the planets nor the Moon makes any major aspects to each other, and on such a day the Moon's course is said to be 'void'. There is nothing wrong with a day like this but there is no point in trying to start anything new or anything important because there isn't enough of a planetary boost to get it off the ground. Stick to your normal routine.

CAPRICORN

MONDAY, 29TH MARCH
Moon square Pluto

There is no point in taking anything at face value today, not unless you want to be ripped off or otherwise messed about. You really need to keep your wits about you and carefully analyse any bits of information that come your way. If thinking of travel, then take care for, as we all know, attractive brochures can be extremely misleading.

TUESDAY, 30TH MARCH
Jupiter trine Pluto

The skeletons are certainly rattling in their closets today! The aspect between Pluto and Jupiter shows that old secrets are about to be blurted out! Shocking these may be, yet it is all to the good in the long run.

WEDNESDAY, 31ST MARCH
Full Moon

Today's Full Moon shows that important decisions have to be made at a time of rapidly changing circumstances. News that arrives today could well be disturbing, yet will prove to be a blessing in disguise in the long run. You may be considering a move of home, possibly to a distant location, or even throwing in your present career to take up an educational course of some kind. People you meet while travelling will have important words to say.

April at a Glance

LOVE	♥	♥	♥
WORK	★		
MONEY	£	£	£
HEALTH	✪	✪	✪
LUCK	♘	♘	

THURSDAY, 1ST APRIL
Sun conjunct Jupiter

Your parents may have good news today, especially in connection with a financial matter. If they have been ill, downhearted or in some kind of mess, then the

CAPRICORN

planets are showing a much more optimistic outlook for the future for them. Your home life should be extremely jolly these days, with parties and events to enjoy in the house and also in and around your neighbourhood.

FRIDAY, 2ND APRIL
Mercury direct

A lot of tension is dissipated as Mercury resumes direct motion today. This is a good chance to resolve misunderstandings, sort out confused thinking and get more mobile. Short trips which lead to happy meetings are the favoured activity today.

SATURDAY, 3RD APRIL
Moon conjunct Mars

Your ideals verge on the revolutionary as the Moon links up with Mars in your house of dreams and aspirations. Not for you quietly mulling over the injustices of this world, you'll want to man the barricades to do something about it. Even if your aspirations don't reach as high as changing the whole world, you'll still have a few tall orders to accomplish. Your anger is likely to be directed at the 'system', but some friends could come in for a little flak too.

SUNDAY, 4TH APRIL
Mercury sextile Venus

You could fall madly, deeply and truly in love today! In fact, if you so much as step outside your own front door, you will be sure to attract at least one interesting member of the opposite sex. If you are already in a happy relationship, then the feelings between you and your lover will deepen and deepen under this planetary aspect.

MONDAY, 5TH APRIL
Moon sextile Neptune

Look at investment options and quiet ways of salting away your money. Your shrewd eye will see the way to future profit. It all bodes well for your financial fortunes in the long term.

TUESDAY, 6TH APRIL
Saturn square Neptune

Today's rare aspect between Saturn and Neptune could be very confusing since you know what needs to be done, but you won't have the faintest idea of how to get started! Take great care, especially with long-term financial affairs. If at all possible, leave these until the planets are more kindly disposed.

CAPRICORN

WEDNESDAY, 7TH APRIL
Sun sextile Uranus

Some good news will wake you up to the possibilities of improvement in your home today. If you're used to huge bills arriving in your hall, then prepare to be surprised and delighted by a financial development that actually puts some more spending power at your disposal. If you're wise, you will turn this windfall into something lasting for your home.

THURSDAY, 8TH APRIL
Moon sextile Mars

Your social life will take off like a rocket today with friends and colleagues inviting you out to all kinds of interesting events. This is a great day on which to shine and to really stand out from the crowd. If, for example, you take part in some kind of sporting or competitive event, you stand a good chance of taking the victor's cup.

FRIDAY, 9TH APRIL
Moon sextile Mercury

Being too proud to talk over a problem is a self-defeating attitude. A relative may find themselves in just such a situation and need encouragement. All you have to do is listen because the problem could well be solved by simply talking about it. Just smile and nod in the appropriate places and you'll both be OK.

SATURDAY, 10TH APRIL
Moon square Saturn

You seem to be right in the middle of a generation gap today. On the one hand, your parents and/or any other parental figures are making one kind of demand upon you, and, on the other hand, your children are driving you insane with their demands. You might as well leave them all to get on with it while you take the dog out for a walk, that is, if the dog is still talking to you!

SUNDAY, 11TH APRIL
Moon sextile Sun

This is an excellent day on which to buy goodies for the home. If your curtains need replacing or if the dog has chewed the cushion covers just one time too many, take yourself out to the shops and see what you can do about it.

MONDAY, 12TH APRIL
Venus into Gemini

Venus moves out of the fun, sun and pleasure area of your chart into the work, duty and health area, and it will stay there for the next few weeks. This suggests

CAPRICORN

that any problems related to work and duty will become easier to handle and that you will start to see some kind of practical outcome from all that you have been doing lately. If you have been off-colour recently, Venus will help you to feel better soon.

TUESDAY, 13TH APRIL
Moon sextile Venus

Younger members of the family will surprise you by welcoming you home with a meal cooked and the house all cleared up. Don't forget to thank them profusely and to show real appreciation of their efforts. A woman may be helpful in connection with a project that you are working on at the moment.

WEDNESDAY, 14TH APRIL
Moon into Aries

Though you've got the usual duties to perform, you'll be happiest in your own home, surrounded by your family today. With the Moon in her own house, it is likely to be a nostalgic time in which you'll want to recall the good old days in the company of those who know you well. You need emotional security now.

THURSDAY, 15TH APRIL
Moon conjunct Jupiter

Some members of your family seem to look at you as a sort of superhero at the moment. While this is rather flattering, it is also inaccurate. You can't actually manage to do everything they would want, no matter how much they expand your ego. Keep a firm grip on reality because if you start believing your own publicity there's no end to the trouble it could cause.

FRIDAY, 16TH APRIL
New Moon

The New Moon falls in the sphere of home and family today, indicating a need for a change. For some reason, you've been dissatisfied with your domestic set-up so you may consider looking at house prices in your own or indeed another area. You probably feel that you need more space and light in your life which your present home isn't providing. A family member may be considering setting up home and deserves all the encouragement you can give.

SATURDAY, 17TH APRIL
Mercury into Aries

The past exerts a powerful influence as Mercury enters the house of heritage. You'll find that things long forgotten will somehow re-enter your life over the

CAPRICORN

next couple of weeks. An interest in your family heritage may develop, or possibly a new-found passion for antiques. Some good, meaningful conversations in the family will prove enlightening.

SUNDAY, 18TH APRIL
Moon conjunct Venus

You can expect women to be a great help to you today and whether these females are relatives, friends or even new acquaintances, they will do a great deal for you. Your female friends and companions will not only be on hand to give you practical help but also to boost your confidence and allow you to talk over a few problems with them.

MONDAY, 19TH APRIL
Mars opposite Saturn

A forceful friend will be determined to get his own way today, but you'd be very foolish to go along with plans that offend your common sense. Be cautious and don't be railroaded into anything!

TUESDAY, 20TH APRIL
Sun into Taurus

You are going to be in a slightly frivolous frame of mind over the next few weeks and you shouldn't punish yourself for this. Pay attention to a creative interest or a demanding hobby, or get involved in something creative on behalf of others. A couple of typical examples would be involvement in the production of a school play or making preparations for a flower and vegetable show.

WEDNESDAY, 21ST APRIL
Venus opposite Pluto

We all have days when we feel under the weather and this looks like being one of those for you. If you are a lady, you may be in for a particularly nasty 'monthly', but either sex may be bothered by a touch of laryngitis or something similar.

THURSDAY, 22ND APRIL
Mercury sextile Neptune

Money worries are set to be eased by the beneficial combination of Neptune and Mercury. You may not see any quick results to this, yet the ball will be set in motion for increased savings and getting more from your insurance and investment policies soon.

CAPRICORN

FRIDAY, 23RD APRIL
Jupiter sextile Uranus

Good news concerning money is on its way to you, thoughtfully provided by Uranus, which, true to form, brings this stroke of good fortune out of the blue! A windfall is likely for some!

SATURDAY, 24TH APRIL
Sun opposite Mars

If you are trying to do something interesting in company with others today, then you may find yourself becoming increasingly frustrated and disappointed by their lack of enthusiasm for your pet project. Friends may suddenly decide to leave you to get on with things alone and you could feel neglected as a result. You may even find yourself in opposition to a group of people.

SUNDAY, 25TH APRIL
Moon trine Saturn

This is a good day for indulging your passions. Any romantic interest or pet hobby will do well as your attention is engaged by a pleasurable expression of your flair. Any ideas you have will now achieve solid form. This marvellous blend of creativity and sound common sense is a winner.

MONDAY, 26TH APRIL
Mercury trine Pluto

This is a good day on which to scan the newspapers and ask your neighbours for ideas. You may want to put these ideas into action in your home or at work, but either way, the decisions that you come to today will be good ones.

TUESDAY, 27TH APRIL
Sun conjunct Saturn

The conjunction of the Sun and Saturn makes the whole question of rules and regulations a pressing issue. If you're dealing with youngsters, then a series of checks and balances must be set up, for everyone's sake. Have you been too lenient, or turned a blind eye to some mischief? Do you believe that the only thing you're teaching is not to get caught? If any of the above are true, then think seriously before the situation gets out of hand.

WEDNESDAY, 28TH APRIL
Moon opposite Mercury

You may have to rush round to see one or other of your parents today. Alternatively, another older member of your circle could need your assistance now. The problem is that the messages that you are being given are a bit muddled and when you actually look into the reality of the situation, it may be much better, or worse, than you first realized.

THURSDAY, 29TH APRIL

Mercury sextile Uranus

Expect friends and neighbours to drop in unexpectedly today. They may bring money-making ideas with them or they may inspire you to do something interesting with your home and your surroundings. A friend may offer to help you with a domestic do-it-yourself type of project.

FRIDAY, 30TH APRIL

Full Moon

Today's Full Moon could make you feel a bit tetchy and tense and it could also bring you some sort of unexpected expense. The best thing to do today is to stick to your usual routine and not start anything new or important. Jog along as usual and try not to become caught up in anybody else's bad mood.

May at a Glance

LOVE	♥	♥	♥	♥	
WORK	★	★	★	★	
MONEY	£	£	£		
HEALTH	⊕	⊕	⊕		
LUCK	∪	∪	∪	∪	∪

SATURDAY, 1ST MAY

Mercury conjunct Jupiter

There could be some more money coming into your home now and this will enable you to make choices that were hitherto impossible. The timing seems to be right for you to strike out on your own and to find a place in which to live or to work that fits in with your character and your current lifestyle.

CAPRICORN

SUNDAY, 2ND MAY
Moon sextile Neptune

Trust your instincts today, especially where your hard-earned cash is concerned. There's every possibility that you can turn a remarkable profit by simple use of your intuition. On the other hand, you can also prevent yourself from losing money since you could smell a dodgy deal a mile away!

MONDAY, 3RD MAY
Moon sextile Uranus

Luck smiles on you today for the mixed rays of the Moon and Uranus boost your cash flow nicely. For many this could mean a windfall. A fortune is not promised, but any amount of money coming your way is better than no money at all. Keep your fingers crossed because you've got astral help to get your own way now. Follow all hunches today.

TUESDAY, 4TH MAY
Moon opposite Venus

Emotional anxieties come to the fore today, but if you were honest, you'd have to admit that you're being slightly neurotic over this. It is all the fault of the Lunar opposition to Venus which has managed to both heighten your emotional vulnerability and sap your energy levels at the same time. This problem of tiredness occurs again and again, so perhaps a visit to your medical practitioner would be in order.

WEDNESDAY, 5TH MAY
Mars into Libra

It is now time for drive, force and ambition, as Mars enters the career area encouraging you to forge ahead with plans. You may feel you want to take a more independent course so this influence favours those who run their own businesses. You'll be very brash and forthright.

THURSDAY, 6TH MAY
Moon square Jupiter

This is not the time for gambling on anything. Stick to tried and tested methods and don't overreach yourself in any way. If you go out on a limb now, you could risk everything that you have worked so hard to achieve and you could lose much that is important to you. You may have to spend some extra money on your home or on a mother figure today.

CAPRICORN

FRIDAY, 7TH MAY
Neptune retrograde

This is not a day to concern yourself with financial dealings, money or purchases of any sort. Neptune charts a backwards course for a while and that will tend to throw any well-ordered monetary planning into total confusion. True to the liquid nature of the planet, money will slip through your fingers like water. You'll be prone to more impulse spending than is usual and that could be disastrous for your domestic budget, so keep a tight grip on the purse strings and your feet firmly on the ground.

SATURDAY, 8TH MAY
Mercury into Taurus

Mercury moves into a part of your horoscope that is concerned with creativity. Mercury rules such things as thinking, learning and communications, but it can also be associated with skills and craftwork of various kinds. The combination of creativity and craftwork suggest that the next few weeks would be a good time to work on hobbies such as dressmaking, carpentry and so on.

SUNDAY, 9TH MAY
Mercury sextile Venus

Your mind and heart seem to be in harmony with each other now. Feelings of loneliness and abandonment will vanish, and you will feel more loved and cherished than you have for a long time.

MONDAY, 10TH MAY
Moon square Pluto

Though you have the tendency today to say exactly what you mean when it would apparently be better to exercise a little tact, it won't do you any real harm. Though you might offend in the short term, the influence of Venus and Jupiter ensures that no lasting damage is done. By the end of the day everyone will know exactly where they stand.

TUESDAY, 11TH MAY
Mercury square Neptune

Something out of the ordinary could shake your self-confidence and habits today. You could be in confusion for a while but don't panic. Let events develop as they will, and then deal with them. Give yourself time.

CAPRICORN

WEDNESDAY, 12TH MAY
Moon trine Pluto

As a relief from pressure, you need some time to unwind and give your pent-up nerves some much needed rest. You won't want to be bothered by inconsequential chatter because you've got to have some peace to get your thoughts in order. Lock the door, take the phone off the hook and enjoy your own company for a change:

THURSDAY, 13TH MAY
Mercury conjunct Saturn

Your thoughts take on a grim turn today as Mercury, planet of the mind, meets Saturn, the harsh taskmaster. Your natural optimism is dulled by the unpromising prospects that face you. All the fun seems to have gone out of your life at the moment. Perhaps you feel that a barrier has sprung up separating you from loved ones. If that's the case, it is better to voice your fears rather than wallow in depression. If you don't speak up now, you'll regret it.

FRIDAY, 14TH MAY
Moon sextile Venus

It is a day of relaxation, but not necessarily of calm. The Lunar aspect of Venus puts you in a sensual mood, determined to enjoy the finer things of life. Good food, good wines and the company of someone you love, are the recipe for perfect bliss. It doesn't matter what you do, as long as you enjoy it. Give yourself over to absolute pleasure today.

SATURDAY, 15TH MAY
New Moon

There's a New Moon today casting a glow over your artistic potential. Your talents should shine so have some belief in yourself and in what you can offer to the world at large. Of course, if art and literature leave you cold, you may be more inclined to an amorous path. Conventional values are not for you since you're determined to be yourself and to chart your own course. Make time to have fun, you deserve it.

SUNDAY, 16TH MAY
Venus sextile Saturn

If there's one thing that's certain in life it is the fact that the path of true love never yet ran smoothly! Today's aspect between Venus and Saturn, both in highly emotional areas of your chart, shows that there are a few storms to weather. However, you could look at this period as a clearing of the air because all

CAPRICORN

outbursts will be short-lived. This should be good for the long-term future of your relationship. Think how much fun it will be making up afterwards.

MONDAY, 17TH MAY
Mercury square Uranus

Having sudden expense dropped into your lap by someone else is not one of your favourite sensations, but that's the way it is today. Some colourful words will be forcibly expressed due to a young person's spending habits.

TUESDAY, 18TH MAY
Moon sextile Saturn

This could be the day when a casual dalliance turns into something far more stable and lasting. Affections that have been growing steadily can now be put on a firmer footing.

WEDNESDAY, 19TH MAY
Moon square Jupiter

Your horizons seem to be shrinking. There are many possible reasons for this kind of situation and one instance may be temporary limitations due to a health problem, while another may be that you have to look after either an older or a younger person in the family for a while. Either way, you won't be able to stray very far just for the moment.

THURSDAY, 20TH MAY
Moon opposite Neptune

'Neither a borrower nor a lender be,' said Shakespeare, and that's good advice for you today. There's a deceptive influence around you so keep a tight grip on the purse strings and don't let your attention waver from financial realities. Don't be taken in by glib promises and fast talkers. There's an ever-present danger that you'll be conned (something that can happen to the best of us). Take extra care of your possessions too.

FRIDAY, 21ST MAY
Sun into Gemini

The Sun moves into your Solar sixth house of work and duty for the next month. This Solar movement will also encourage you to concentrate on your health and well-being and also that of your family. If you are off-colour, the Sun will help you to get back to full health once again. If you have jobs that need to be done, the next month or so will be a good time to get them done.

CAPRICORN

SATURDAY, 22ND MAY
Uranus retrograde

Though it may be a bind, the retrograde motion of Uranus from today makes you go over your financial arrangements with a fine-tooth comb. You may want to charge ahead with loans, purchases and luxuries, yet it would be an excellent idea to know exactly where you stand. Be prepared to check over your figures because attention paid to cash affairs now will save a lot of trouble later.

SUNDAY, 23RD MAY
Mercury into Gemini

The movement of Mercury into your Solar sixth house of work, duties and health suggests that a slightly more serious phase is on the way. Over the next three weeks or so you will have to concentrate on what needs to be done rather than on having a good time. You may have a fair bit to do with neighbours, colleagues and relatives of around your own age group soon and you will have to spend some time on the phone with them.

MONDAY, 24TH MAY
Moon trine Mercury

If you have been feeling frustrated and unable to get any sense out of anybody, today's excellent aspect between the Moon and Mercury will sweep all that away. You will be able to make great strides at work, or in any kind of setting where an appreciation of your status and authority make the wheels turn smoothly.

TUESDAY, 25TH MAY
Sun trine Neptune

You are able to dip into a pool of inspiration now. Your dreams seem set to become a practical reality and success is on the way. If you are planning a visit to the shops or to any kind of tourist area, keep your eyes open because you will probably be able to pick up something that really enhances your life or that lifts your spirits just by owning it.

WEDNESDAY, 26TH MAY
Sun conjunct Mercury

You will be a source of wonder today as you effortlessly tackle anything and everything that the world can throw at you. The Sun's conjunction with Mercury puts a powerful emphasis on your house of work so this is the time to improve your prospects and generally make your way up the ladder of success. This is a good day to attend interviews and otherwise get your ideas a fair hearing. You can't afford to sit back and wait any longer. Don't hide your light under a bushel.

CAPRICORN

THURSDAY, 27TH MAY
Moon square Neptune

There is nothing you'd like better than to have some social fun today; however you may not be able to indulge yourself because the bank balance is overstretched.

FRIDAY, 28TH MAY
Moon square Uranus

A friend's pleas for financial assistance could ring alarm bells. Though he or she may seem genuine enough there's a nagging doubt at the back of your mind. Perhaps you suspect that any money that goes that way will not end up where it's intended to go. There may be a need for cash to service a secret vice such as gambling or alcohol abuse. Be firm and refuse to help on this occasion; plead poverty yourself if it helps you out of a jam.

SATURDAY, 29TH MAY
Mars opposite Jupiter

Luck is definitely not with you so avoid taking chances today. Don't lend money to anyone, you won't see it back. Don't enter any kind of business or family arrangement that you aren't happy with and don't accept that invitation to go bungee jumping either!

SUNDAY, 30TH MAY
Full Moon

Apart from a slightly frustrating Full Moon situation today, there is not much going on in the planetary firmament. The best thing to do is to stick to your usual way of doing things and to avoid starting anything new or important. If you feel off-colour or out of sorts, then take whatever medicines you need and try not to work too hard.

MONDAY, 31ST MAY
Venus square Mars

This is going to be a difficult day because it becomes increasingly obvious that your life is more tangled than a bowl of spaghetti. Your career seems at odds with the domestic situation, which in turn complicates affairs of the heart. You may feel like a juggler trying to keep too many balls in the air at once. To handle this situation you need delicacy and tact, so start practising!

CAPRICORN

June at a Glance

LOVE	♥	♥	♥	♥	♥
WORK	★				
MONEY	£	£			
HEALTH	✪	✪	✪		
LUCK	♘				

TUESDAY, 1ST JUNE
Venus square Jupiter

You will find it hard to keep the peace in the home today. Your partner and your parents (or his parents) are at loggerheads. Nothing you can do will put things right. You can only wait for them to get over their bad moods.

WEDNESDAY, 2ND JUNE
Sun opposite Pluto

If there's one thing you can't stand it is a petty dictator. Unfortunately, that's exactly what you're set to run into today. This encounter could well leave you seething inside but it isn't wise to lose your temper. Think about your revenge first because a clever turn of words will have more effect than a fiery storming from the field of battle.

THURSDAY, 3RD JUNE
Mars direct

Any professional obstacles that have stood in your path should now dissipate as the direct motion of the planet Mars adds tremendous energy to your drive to the top. There are few who could match your capacity for hard work now. So use this boost in vitality to good effect and get the job well done.

FRIDAY, 4TH JUNE
Mercury trine Mars

Good advice received today should be followed to the letter. An influential person can see that you're going places and will do his utmost to smooth your path. However, you mustn't be too impulsive, and accept all criticism and guidance with good grace. It is OK to be straight to the point, an approach which wins respect, but be circumspect in your actions and take your lead from someone who knows the game better than you.

SATURDAY, 5TH JUNE
Venus into Leo

Venus enters the area of your chart that is closely involved with love and sex today. Oddly enough, this aspect can bring the end of a difficult relationship or, just as easily, begin a wonderful new one. If you have been dating but haven't yet got around to 'mating', this could be the start of something wonderful. Your emotional life over the next two or three weeks should be something to remember, that's for sure!

SUNDAY, 6TH JUNE
Moon square Pluto

You're in a vague, distant mood today; completely out of tune with those around you. You float through life in a dream world refusing to admit anything discordant and ugly. Of course, the nasty side of life doesn't go away simply by ignoring its existence. You will have to face unpleasant facts eventually; you just cannot manage to do so now.

MONDAY, 7TH JUNE
Mercury into Cancer

The inquisitive Mercury moves into your Solar house of marriage and long-lasting relationships from today, ushering in a period when a renewed understanding can be reached between yourself and your partner. New relationships can be formed under this influence too, though these will tend to be on a light, fairly superficial level. Good humour and plenty of charm should be a feature for a few weeks, though you must try to curb a tendency to needlessly criticize another's foibles. Remember, not even you are perfect!

TUESDAY, 8TH JUNE
Sun trine Uranus

A totally unexpected turn of events is likely today. In work affairs, movements further up the ladder of command could have a beneficial influence on your own position. More money is likely to come in soon.

WEDNESDAY, 9TH JUNE
Moon sextile Uranus

It is time to take a good long look at the state of your home. Has your attention been so distracted that you haven't noticed the imperfections that are marring the

CAPRICORN

general effect of your abode? If so, then this is your chance to do something about it. The stars show that you have sufficient cash to get your home into a good state of repair, so what are you waiting for?

THURSDAY, 10TH JUNE
Venus opposite Neptune

The opposition of Venus and Neptune sounds warning bells. It is obvious that your personal taste is at an all-time high but your judgement may be sorely lacking. A beautiful object you consider buying may not be all it seems so don't be persuaded otherwise. It's a good rule of thumb not to judge by surface appearances today. Any antiques in your possession may be worth more than you know so don't part with them without taking independent advice.

FRIDAY, 11TH JUNE
Moon square Uranus

Temptation abounds today, making you a danger to your bank balance if you're allowed anywhere near a shopping mall. You've got the best intentions of course, thinking of a gift for a child or romantic partner, rather than treating yourself. You are generous but you have to stay within a budget. A small but tasteful item would do, rather than spending a fortune on something ostentatious that will probably be unsuitable anyway.

SATURDAY, 12TH JUNE
Moon trine Neptune

Every single practical thought and intention has flown under the influence of the Moon and Neptune. The sensitivity of this planetary combination enhances your imagination but also promotes fantasy and idle dreaming. That's all well and good if you've got nothing important to do, but if there are any vital tasks to accomplish, you'll have some trouble keeping in touch with reality long enough to get them off the ground. It might be best to leave financial and business matters to another day.

SUNDAY, 13TH JUNE
New Moon

Today's New Moon gives you the stamina to shrug off any minor ailments that have been troubling you. Occurring, as it does, in your Solar house of health and work, it is obvious that you need to get yourself into shape to face the challenges that await you. A few early nights, a better diet and a readiness to give up bad habits such as smoking, will work wonders.

CAPRICORN

MONDAY, 14TH JUNE
Venus trine Pluto

You and your lover seem to be making a deeper and more meaningful commitment to each other now. A relationship that was not much more than a mere flirtation seems to be far more important to both of you. Deep and intimate feelings of need and desire are taking you and your heart over.

TUESDAY, 15TH JUNE
Mercury sextile Saturn

What a heavenly day! Love is in the air and deep feelings of harmony and togetherness will bring you and your partner closer together than ever. Plan a warm, sexy, romantic and loving evening together.

WEDNESDAY, 16TH JUNE
Sun trine Mars

There's no stopping you today as you've got more than enough energy to get everything done and in shipshape order. Even if you have to put in a little overtime, it will be no hardship, since you're determined to get your current tasks under control before you move on to more interesting projects. This vitality can't fail to do your career prospects good.

THURSDAY, 17TH JUNE
Moon opposite Uranus

You may think that you know best when it comes to money but are you being a little hasty? Even though it goes against the grain, it would be a good idea to get some advice from someone who specializes in money management. If your idea of cash is that it is for spending, it could be time to look at pensions and insurance schemes, boring though they may be. If you're in any doubt, then ask a person in the know.

FRIDAY, 18TH JUNE
Moon trine Jupiter

This should be a pleasant day with some rather nice surprises both at home and in the world outside your home. Your partner may cheer you up by suggesting that you book a holiday or that you plan a pleasant trip of some kind. There may be a bit more money on its way into the family coffers, or you may find that your debts are not as great as you had expected.

CAPRICORN

SATURDAY, 19TH JUNE
Venus square Saturn

It is important that you take nothing for granted now. Your luck has temporarily deserted you, especially in emotional affairs, so make sure you don't harp on about the past. Where intense feelings are concerned it is definitely one to let sleeping dogs lie. A good relationship is worth working at, and if that involves putting old injuries out of your mind, then so be it.

SUNDAY, 20TH JUNE
Sun sextile Jupiter

There is a feeling of luck and opportunity around you. If illness has plagued you recently, then you should now start to feel much better. The same goes for other members of your family. There will be new contacts to be made and new opportunities finding their way to your doorstep both at work and at home.

MONDAY, 21ST JUNE
Sun into Cancer

The Sun moves into the area of your chart devoted to relationships from today. If things have been difficult in a partnership, either personal or in business, then this is your chance to put everything back into its proper place. It is obvious that the significant other in your life deserves respect and affection and that's just what you're now prepared to give. Teamwork is the key to success over the next month.

TUESDAY, 22ND JUNE
Venus opposite Uranus

This is one of those days when the heart definitely rules the head! You will be prone to sudden uncontrollable passions as your sexual urges reach fever pitch!

WEDNESDAY, 23RD JUNE
Mercury square Mars

So much to do and so little time at your disposal! That's the way you feel today as a mountain of tasks awaits your attention. Your partner, too, may be extra demanding and you simply have to make time to fit everything in. The advice is, 'Don't panic!' You can get around everything with a little forethought. Organize your time sensibly.

THURSDAY, 24TH JUNE
Moon opposite Saturn

Don't be too downhearted if an event you've been looking forward to is cancelled

CAPRICORN

or postponed. There is a reason for everything, even if it is not apparent now. Equally, you shouldn't be too ready to take on any extra burdens today. You've got enough to cope with already, and if you were relying on help, you can forget it. Other people will be too caught up in their own concerns to render any assistance to you!

FRIDAY, 25TH JUNE
Mercury square Jupiter

There seems to be a measure of disagreement around you over money matters today. Some members of your family may consider that others shouldn't be spending what they want to spend, or that they should be spending their money in a different way or on other things. You may be accused, too, of being too profligate with the pennies (or cents, dollars or anything else that you can get your sticky little hands on)!

SATURDAY, 26TH JUNE
Mercury into Leo

Mercury moves into one of the most sensitive areas of your chart from today. Anything of an intimate nature, from your physical relationships to the state of your bank balance, comes under scrutiny. Turn your heightened perceptions to your love life, important partnerships, and any affair that deals with investment, insurance, tax or shared resources. An intelligent approach now will save you a lot of problems later.

SUNDAY, 27TH JUNE
Moon trine Venus

Take the opportunity to show your loved ones how much you care today and if you accompany your remarks with a gift of flowers or chocolates, so much the better. This will all be well received and much appreciated by your loved one, perhaps reviving your sex life. Well, it's worth a try, isn't it?

MONDAY, 28TH JUNE
Jupiter into Taurus

The movement of Jupiter into your Solar area of luxury and fun will expand your capacity for pleasure to the point where it becomes sheer self-indulgence. You'll now be extra affectionate, generous and outgoing, with a strong sense of pride.

TUESDAY, 29TH JUNE
Moon trine Saturn

Any creative project that you have been working at will begin to fall into place.

CAPRICORN

You may decide to take an interest in music or other artistic pursuits, so sign on at your local college for those guitar lessons today!

WEDNESDAY, 30TH JUNE
Mercury opposite Neptune

An opposition between Mercury, the planet of mentality, and Neptune, planet of dreams, will make it hard for you to concentrate fully on anything today. Despite this mental mist, you may well experience some very meaningful thoughts and dreams.

July at a Glance

LOVE	♥	♥	♥	
WORK	★	★		
MONEY	£	£	£	£
HEALTH	☉			
LUCK	♘	♘		

THURSDAY, 1ST JULY
Moon sextile Pluto

Your inner world seems so much more vivid than mundane reality just now. Your dreams and fantasies give you an insight into a far richer, more meaningful existence. Take note of your nocturnal ramblings because within your world of sleep there lie answers to many of your problems. It is obvious that your unconscious mind is trying to pass on a message so try to listen to the small voice of your intuition. Don't ignore your hunches, because they're likely to be spot on especially where money is concerned.

FRIDAY, 2ND JULY
Moon opposite Venus

You may want to be the last of the big spenders today but it is not really a good idea. You may need to consult an accountant or your bank manager in order to see what you can or cannot get away with during the months ahead. There is no doubt about it, whether you have only yourself to answer to or whether you are part of any kind of partnership, you will have to cut down on the luxuries for a while.

CAPRICORN

SATURDAY, 3RD JULY
Moon trine Mars

Be prepared for an action-packed social life today. The Moon and Mars unite to propel you into a party atmosphere. You could wear less hardy souls out because you'll be in a dancing mood determined to have a lot of fun. If you haven't got anything special to celebrate, then make something up and invite your friends along. A good time will be had by all.

SUNDAY, 4TH JULY
Mars opposite Jupiter

If you ask a friend to act as a go-between in a delicate matter of love, things will go completely wrong! It seems destined that the object of your affections is going to misconstrue all that he or she is told.

MONDAY, 5TH JULY
Mars into Scorpio

You're caught up in a crusading zeal as Mars enters your Solar house of ideals and aspirations from today. A worthy cause that has interested you for some time will take on an added gloss as you prepare to do your utmost on its behalf. Injustice of any kind won't be tolerated for you are keen to stand up to any authority to defend the rights of those less fortunate than yourself. Your friends will have cause to be grateful for your unswerving loyalty in the weeks ahead. The only warning implicit in this transit is to remember to look before you leap impulsively into the fray.

TUESDAY, 6TH JULY
Moon square Sun

You aren't in the most active of moods today. The Moon's square aspect to the Sun ensures that you'll be happiest within your home environment. You won't want to tax your system, so a day of lounging about is your idea of bliss. Of course, there are domestic duties too, but you're likely to rely on the goodwill of your other half to do them. Don't be surprised if your lazy attitude is resented.

WEDNESDAY, 7TH JULY
Moon trine Venus

A truly romantic interlude could turn into real passion today. You seem to have the kind of magnetic charisma that's guaranteed to make you irresistible to the opposite sex. Even if all you end up doing is sitting about at home with your loved one, make this as sexy and loving an occasion as you can. Set the scene with perfume, dim lights and sexy music tonight!

CAPRICORN

THURSDAY, 8TH JULY
Mercury trine Pluto

Your powers of intuition are reaching a new high today and you may even find yourself experiencing something on the psychic or spiritual level. Inner thoughts and feelings seem to be more important to you than the workaday world.

FRIDAY, 9TH JULY
Moon square Venus

There is an intimate feel to today's stars as the Moon and Venus are in aspect from romantic and sexual areas of your horoscope. This could herald a passionate embrace, which if not wise, is certainly enjoyable. In financial affairs, try not to spend too much on pleasure just now.

SATURDAY, 10TH JULY
Moon sextile Mercury

As the Moon contacts Mercury, it is time to put your cards on the table. A meeting will work in your favour if you are open and honest in your opinions. Don't be afraid to stand out from the crowd.

SUNDAY, 11TH JULY
Mars square Neptune

A demanding friend will get on your nerves today. No sooner do you settle on one course of action than the other person will decide that it is boring and want to do something else.

MONDAY, 12TH JULY
Mercury retrograde

Life is always difficult when Mercury turns to retrograde motion but the good news (if it is good) is that everyone else will be affected in the same way that you are. Over the next few weeks, messages will fail to arrive, business and money matters may become fouled up or delayed, and if you have to use a computer or any other kind of business machinery, it will be taken over by gremlins!

TUESDAY, 13TH JULY
New Moon

The only planetary activity today is a New Moon in your opposite sign. It is possible that this could bring the start of a new relationship for the lonely, but to be honest, this planetary aspect is a bit too weak for such a big event. It is much more likely that you will improve on a current relationship rather than start a new one at this time.

CAPRICORN

WEDNESDAY, 14TH JULY
Moon conjunct Mercury

A declaration of love is certain today as the Moon conjuncts Mercury in your house of passion. This could be the start of something truly spectacular in your love life. You'll be able to talk freely about the most intimate needs and desires. There is no room for embarrassment when there's such harmony between two people.

THURSDAY, 15TH JULY
Venus trine Jupiter

If you aren't already on your vacation, you won't see any reason why you shouldn't plan a break that will refresh your spirits and indulge your sense of adventure. The two most fortunate planets, Venus and Jupiter, are in splendid aspect today, giving you the impulse to fly off to exotic places and happily cast off the cares of the world. Immerse yourself in pleasure; it doesn't sound like a bad idea.

FRIDAY, 16TH JULY
Mercury trine Pluto

Secrets are the main theme of the day. You should not be too ready to impart confidences now or to be too trusting. Some things are best kept to yourself especially where money is concerned.

SATURDAY, 17TH JULY
Void Moon

The Moon is 'void of course' today, so don't bother with anything important and don't start anything new. Stick to your usual routines and don't change your lifestyle in any way.

SUNDAY, 18TH JULY
Saturn square Uranus

Money and the lack of it are the main problems of the day. Saturn conspires with Uranus to provide you with unexpected expense which will restrict your capacity to have fun.

MONDAY, 19TH JULY
Moon trine Uranus

You may wonder if you're on the right road today since the Lunar aspect to Uranus urges you to re-examine your old values and ambitions. You probably feel that you aren't getting enough satisfaction from your work so you'll be busy looking around for a new position which will provide more self-esteem and financial reward.

CAPRICORN

TUESDAY, 20TH JULY
Moon square Sun

This is one of those days when you wish you had stayed in bed! There are potential difficulties all around you now and it will take all your attempts at tact and charm to get others to behave decently. All those who should, by rights, be on your side will lack any urge to co-operate and your usual sources of sympathy will have run out of the milk of human kindness.

WEDNESDAY, 21ST JULY
Jupiter square Neptune

Promises of repayment are likely to be outright lies, so don't rely on a friend coming up trumps for you. Financial affairs in general are on dodgy ground today so be realistic about your chances and don't gamble!

THURSDAY, 22ND JULY
Mercury square Mars

When you boil with fury, everyone around had better watch out because you aren't noted for a forgiving nature. Ill-considered words are to blame for your inner turmoil. A tactless remark could wound you deeply. However, not all comments are directed at you personally so don't assume that associates know more about your private life than they actually do. You could turn a conjecture into a certainty if you over-react.

FRIDAY, 23RD JULY
Sun into Leo

Today, the Sun enters your Solar eighth house of beginnings and endings. Thus, over the next month, you can expect something to wind its way to a conclusion, while something else starts to take its place. This doesn't seem to signify a major turning point or any really big event in your life, but it does mark one of those small changes that we all go through from time to time.

SATURDAY, 24TH JULY
Moon sextile Uranus

Though you are prone to confusion today, this will not be too much of a handicap. For once, life is undemanding, so you can revel in your vagueness for a while.

SUNDAY, 25TH JULY
Mercury square Jupiter

Though you aren't likely to achieve very much today, the combination of Mercury and Jupiter puts you in a good humour, able to see the funny side of nearly anything. Even news that would have disturbed you can be amusing, especially if you half-expected it anyway. At least you know where you stand. In fact, a minor mishap could propel you along a course that you hadn't previously considered, one that will be better for you in the long run.

MONDAY, 26TH JULY
Sun opposite Neptune

Any dealings with money, from high-flying stocks and shares to the small change in your purse, are in dangerous territory today. Your judgement is not at its best and you could so easily make a serious mistake. There are some unscrupulous people in this world so you'd do well to avoid glib talkers who have their eyes on your savings. When dealing with contracts and financial agreements examine the small print extra carefully. Let caution be your watchword and look after the pennies.

TUESDAY, 27TH JULY
Sun square Jupiter

You may think that you're home and dry today, but nothing could be further from the truth. The Sun/Jupiter combination encourages you to take the optimistic view but the realities don't match up with your expectations. If emotional contentment is an issue, it may seem that everything in the garden is lovely but a partner could be concealing a deep dissatisfaction. In financial affairs too, let caution be your watchword.

WEDNESDAY, 28TH JULY
Full Moon eclipse

Something will come to a head today and this may even cause an argument amongst family members. There may have been disagreements over money recently and now it seems that these simmering disagreements are destined to reach the boil. You must stand your ground and prevent others from manipulating you into actions that will work against your best long-term interests.

THURSDAY, 29TH JULY
Moon square Saturn

Monetary security is the troublesome subject today. The Moon makes a harsh aspect to Saturn which puts a damper on many of your favourite pastimes. Perhaps a hobby is proving too expensive, or extravagant meals and nights out are proving a terrible drain on your resources. Tighten the belt for a while, at least until you've got the cash flow under control. You know it makes sense.

CAPRICORN

FRIDAY, 30TH JULY
Sun trine Pluto

You can use a lot of influence in a subtle way at the moment. If you think that those around you are heading in the wrong direction, the odd hint here and there will soon redirect them onto the correct path. You are likely to be a master of applied psychology just now and you will not lose out by the exercise of this remarkable talent.

SATURDAY, 31ST JULY
Mercury into Cancer

Mercury returns to your partnership area for a short while from today. This gives you another chance to have deep, heartfelt conversations with your loved one. Short journeys made together will be very fulfilling.

August at a Glance

LOVE	♥	♥	♥	
WORK	★			
MONEY	£	£	£	
HEALTH	✪	✪	✪	✪
LUCK	♘	♘		

SUNDAY, 1ST AUGUST
Moon trine Mercury

This is likely to be a very busy day and you could find yourself running around like a headless chicken! Other people will expect you to act on their behalf – while you don't mind, it will be hard for you to find a moment to yourself. There could be some extremely interesting news for your partner or for others close to you.

MONDAY, 2ND AUGUST
Moon trine Sun

A marvellous day for pouring oil on troubled waters and calming down ruffled feelings. Any family quarrels can now be placed firmly in the past. A renewed understanding and appreciation of everyone's viewpoint will go a long way to restoring harmony in your home.

CAPRICORN

TUESDAY, 3RD AUGUST
Venus trine Jupiter

A great day for travel and to stretch the boundaries of your experience. Venus and Jupiter team up to provide plenty of opportunities for adventure. Even if you aren't off on a worldwide trek, you can have as much adventure in an intellectual sense.

WEDNESDAY, 4TH AUGUST
Moon trine Venus

This is not a day for duty. The Lunar aspect to Venus puts a romantic spark in your soul. There's nothing you'd like better than an intimate *tête-à-tête* with someone you love. Forget your worries, for today at least, and take that special person in your life out for a night of glamour. If you haven't got a special person, go for glamour anyway. Someone will catch your eye.

THURSDAY, 5TH AUGUST
Moon conjunct Saturn

There is an aura of gloom today as the Moon makes contact with Saturn. All your thoughts are tinged with despair for nothing seems to be going right and you feel isolated and misunderstood. Of course, the truth is somewhat different, and more positive, but you can't see that the grim outlook is of your own making. Try to talk this out with someone you trust; it is better than suffering in silence.

FRIDAY, 6TH AUGUST
Mercury direct

Another sign that relationship difficulties are being resolved is given by Mercury today. The tiny planet takes up a forward course and in doing so, opens lines of communication that have been blocked. Misunderstandings can now be clearly and decisively sorted out.

SATURDAY, 7TH AUGUST
Sun square Mars

You may feel that you are being asked to choose between your friends and your partner today. Think over what is being asked of you and work out if this is reasonable or not. A friend may be too keen to bend your ear on the phone, keeping you from your family for hours on end. On the other hand, your partner may be unreasonably possessive.

SUNDAY, 8TH AUGUST
Sun opposite Uranus

Anything could happen today! The Sun is in opposition to the erratic planet

CAPRICORN

Uranus and that spells an overturning of preconceptions and surprises all the way. Unfortunately, this influence occurs in the financial areas of your chart so some disruption to your cash flow is inevitable. Unconventional answers to money problems are probably the right ones to follow.

MONDAY, 9TH AUGUST
Moon sextile Saturn

If you've been involved in a casual love affair, it may be time to put such a dalliance on a more permanent footing. For some, the big question may be popped!

TUESDAY, 10TH AUGUST
Sun square Saturn

Trying to follow your mood is a bit like riding a roller coaster today. The Sun is in a harsh aspect to Saturn which puts a damper on any plans you have for leisure activities. Duty calls and your instant reaction is vital if you're to sort things out. Fun has to be postponed, which is irritating, yet if you don't deal with necessities you'll have far more to complain about in the long run.

WEDNESDAY, 11TH AUGUST
New Moon eclipse

Even though Nostradamus predicted doom and destruction for today, Sasha and Jonathan are still optimistic. There is a New Moon eclipse in the area of your chart which is devoted to joint matters today. This could make you face up to the fact that one joint arrangement is no longer viable. It may be a business partnership or a personal relationship that is causing trouble and you may reach the unhappy conclusion that this cannot go on any longer. It is possible to change a bad situation but you will have to do so firmly rather than to simply hope that it will get better all by itself.

THURSDAY, 12TH AUGUST
Mercury into Leo

Mercury moves into your Solar eighth house today and it will stay there for the next couple of weeks. This means that you should try to sort out taxes, legacies, alimony, business and corporate matters, insurance documents and any other kind of legal or official papers that relate to your finances. Don't neglect these matters now.

FRIDAY, 13TH AUGUST
Mercury opposite Neptune

Try to avoid signing anything important or agreeing to anything binding today.

CAPRICORN

Your mind is not at its best and you could become embroiled in something that is not in your best interests.

SATURDAY, 14TH AUGUST
Mars opposite Saturn

You'd be a fool if you allowed a wilful friend to get his own way today. Dig your heels in and don't be forced into any course of action that you know in your heart is stupid.

SUNDAY, 15TH AUGUST
Venus into Leo

Venus makes a return visit to your Solar house of sexuality today. This is bound to mean that the libido gets a powerful boost and that your capacity for sensuality soars.

MONDAY, 16TH AUGUST
Moon sextile Sun

Your inner feelings are very much in harmony with everything that is going on around you today. You feel that your bosses and colleagues are on the right track and that you are doing exactly the right thing for your career.

TUESDAY, 17TH AUGUST
Mercury square Jupiter

Having a carefree attitude is generally a good thing, but not today! There's paperwork to be done, serious issues to be attended to and financial institutions to be dealt with. You'll have to force yourself to knuckle down!

WEDNESDAY, 18TH AUGUST
Moon opposite Saturn

From exuberance you are likely to fall into a pit of despondency today. Under the Mercury/Saturn opposition, a friend could cast a wet blanket over your mood by pointing out how far you have to go to achieve your desires. Don't be too downhearted though; hasn't it occurred to you that this genuine concern may be too negative? The truth lies somewhere between your optimism and your friend's warnings. It is up to you to find the balance.

THURSDAY, 19TH AUGUST
Pluto direct

Many of your deep anxieties will be seen in a totally different light from today for Pluto returns to a direct course now. Any psychological blockages or phobias

CAPRICORN

you've experienced will now be easier to deal with. Pay particular attention to dreams and hunches because this is a case of your unconscious mind trying to communicate an important message. You would do well to note the changes in your inner world.

FRIDAY, 20TH AUGUST
Sun conjunct Venus

This should be an easy day because the Sun and Venus fall into line and ensure that everything else does too. You don't have to put much effort in to make all the pieces of your life fit together perfectly. From passionate love affairs to complex financial dealings, your luck is in. Women around you will be very helpful.

SATURDAY, 21ST AUGUST
Moon trine Venus

There is a very sexy moon rising today! Your mood is romantic, loving and very physical. So get close to your lover and show your feelings in the time-honoured way. Plan a loving evening in with plenty of bubbles in the champagne and in the bath water! Cuddle up on the sofa and let the world and its troubles glide past the pair of you for once.

SUNDAY, 22ND AUGUST
Moon trine Jupiter

This should be a highly optimistic day. The Moon is in aspect to Jupiter which always lightens your mood and shows you the world from a more positive viewpoint. Your popularity is guaranteed because when you smile everyone around you will smile too. Good humour is infectious. You've got no time for worry or boring duties. Enjoyment is the keynote of the day, and you'll be determined to make the most of it. Any dealings with children will keep you very happy indeed, and make you feel youthful.

MONDAY, 23RD AUGUST
Sun into Virgo

The Sun moves into your Solar ninth house today and it will stay there for a month. This would be a good time to travel overseas or to explore new neighbourhoods. It is also a good time to take up an interest in spiritual matters. You may find yourself keen to read about religious or philosophical subjects or even to explore the world of psychic healing over the next month or so.

CAPRICORN

TUESDAY, 24TH AUGUST
Venus square Mars

You're likely to be swept off your feet by a new attraction today. Someone you meet in a social setting could give you palpitations; this could be the start of a passionate whirlwind romance. Of course, he or she may not really be your true soulmate since the attraction seems to be totally sexual in nature. However, you'll both have fun in finding out. Passions of all sorts run high at the moment, so you can also expect an explosion of jealousy amongst your friends.

WEDNESDAY, 25TH AUGUST
Jupiter retrograde

Jupiter turns to retrograde motion today and this will slow down all your creative ventures for the time being. This may not be so bad because it will force you to reassess your current activities and to work out other ways of approaching things.

THURSDAY, 26TH AUGUST
Full Moon

This is likely to be a really awkward day for the kind of travelling that you have to do. A vehicle could let you down just when you most need it or the public transport that you usually rely on could suddenly disappear from the face of the earth.

FRIDAY, 27TH AUGUST
Mercury conjunct Venus

You have the ability to charm the birds from the trees today, and better still to charm your lover into doing almost anything that you want. Take some time off to be together to talk, make love or simply enjoy being with each other.

SATURDAY, 28TH AUGUST
Sun trine Jupiter

The astral outlook is tremendously positive at the moment. The aspect between the Sun and Jupiter points the way to good times ahead. Since this splendid event triggers two of the most pleasurable areas of your chart, you'll be filled with expectation and optimism. Creatively you'll be brimming with excellent ideas, while you find that you've got the energy and desire to go out to promote yourself. This is the start of an adventure, but you have to remember that there's bound to be some hard work involved in it somewhere, even if it is not today.

SUNDAY, 29TH AUGUST
Moon trine Pluto

This is a difficult day in the family circle, and though you are aware of the deep

CAPRICORN

feelings involved, you mustn't expect any sudden solutions to long-standing worries. You aren't totally blameless in all of this either. Perhaps bad experiences in the past have forced you to be overly cautious or oppressive. If you can accept the causes of your feelings, then you are one step nearer to resolving them.

MONDAY, 30TH AUGUST
Saturn retrograde

Your Solar house of romance is severely afflicted by Saturn today and it looks as though your illusions have now fled and you may follow them out of the door. A possessive or over-demanding lover might find him or herself high and dry as you jet off to a more congenial emotional climate.

TUESDAY, 31ST AUGUST
Mercury into Virgo

Mercury enters your Solar house of adventure and philosophy from today and stimulates your curiosity. Everything from international affairs to religious questions will tax your mind. Your desire to travel will be boosted for a few weeks, as indeed will a need to expand your knowledge, perhaps by taking up a course at a local college. Keep an open mind. Allow yourself encounters with new ideas.

September at a Glance

LOVE	♥	♥	♥	♥	
WORK	★	★	★	★	★
MONEY	£				
HEALTH	✪	✪	✪		
LUCK	♘	♘	♘	♘	♘

WEDNESDAY, 1ST SEPTEMBER
Moon square Venus

You will hardly have a moment to yourself today. People around you demand your patience and your time. It is good to have friends, but there are times when you wish that they'd all just go away, even if only for five minutes. If you really can't stand the incessant calls on your good nature, pretend to be out!

CAPRICORN

THURSDAY, 2ND SEPTEMBER
Mars into Sagittarius

You seem to be entering a placid and peaceful backwater just now because Mars is disappearing into the quietest area of your chart. However, this is not altogether true because you will spend this reflective time working out what you want from life and making preparations for your future. This is a good time to repay any loans or to fulfil outstanding obligations towards others.

FRIDAY, 3RD SEPTEMBER
Mercury trine Jupiter

Brilliant ideas will turn into concrete reality today so follow your hunches and put your courage to the test. Travel of all kinds is extremely well starred, so shut the door behind you and take to the road.

SATURDAY, 4TH SEPTEMBER
Mercury square Pluto

Accounts, forms, contracts and documents are irritatingly complex today. You seem to have a mental block when it comes to signing your name on the dotted line – and that's the easy bit. When it comes to intricate detail and searching questions you'll wonder why any official has the right to know in the first place. Mentally, you're a bit muddled so try to leave anything too taxing for another day.

SUNDAY, 5TH SEPTEMBER
Moon sextile Saturn

You may find that light flirtation has all the potential of turning into something far more serious under the influence of the Moon and Saturn. Casual relationships can now develop into true commitment.

MONDAY, 6TH SEPTEMBER
Mars sextile Neptune

Your financial strategy should be superb today. A couple of hours spent with a calculator and a notebook will work wonders when budgeting or working out a tax bill.

TUESDAY, 7TH SEPTEMBER
Moon opposite Uranus

You're prone to taking the negative view financially today. No matter how sensibly you have sorted money affairs out, you still believe the worst-case scenario. The chances are that you're being overcautious at the moment so try to see the real prospects as they emerge. They can't possibly be as bad as you imagine.

CAPRICORN

WEDNESDAY, 8TH SEPTEMBER
Sun conjunct Mercury

If you have any kind of legal or official matter to deal with, this would be a good day to get on with it. It is a good time to sign contracts or agreements or to make a business deal. You seem to be taking a deep interest in spiritual matters now and this may be the start of something which will affect the course of your life from here on.

THURSDAY, 9TH SEPTEMBER
New Moon

The New Moon in your house of adventure urges you to push ahead with new projects. You're in a self-confident mood, and feel able to tackle anything the world throws at you. The lure of exotic and far-off places exerts a powerful attraction. Think again about widening your personal horizons by travel or, indeed, by taking up an educational course. Intellectually, you're on top form and your curiosity is boundless.

FRIDAY, 10TH SEPTEMBER
Sun trine Saturn

Better than anyone, you know that it takes more than a good idea to get a big project off the ground. Edison said that 'genius is one per cent inspiration and ninety-nine per cent perspiration,' and you're well aware that effort has to be put into anything worthwhile. At least you're under no illusions. While we're on the subject of clichés, it is also true that a journey of a thousand miles starts with a single step. You are the one to make that step and with determination you will achieve your goal. Do not give up!

SATURDAY, 11TH SEPTEMBER
Venus direct

Venus returns to a more direct path today, promising that an intimate or financial matter that has been troubling can now be dealt with in an open, yet sensitive, manner. You may also find that you develop a powerfully attractive charisma.

SUNDAY, 12TH SEPTEMBER
Moon sextile Venus

Though you have some faults, meanness isn't among them. You will prove that statement today because you'll be determined not to stint on any luxury or enjoyment. A day out with the family could be expensive but it is also going to be fun.

CAPRICORN

MONDAY, 13TH SEPTEMBER
Moon square Neptune

One or more of your so-called friends could have the intention of taking you for a financial ride today. You'd be daft to go along with anything that makes too large a hole in your pocket. You have been warned!

TUESDAY, 14TH SEPTEMBER
Moon opposite Saturn

You may be concerned by a youngster's problems today. Confidence is low and it will be up to you to inject some enthusiasm back into a flagging spirit. You know that all this child needs is a good talking to, but the direct approach is likely to be counter-productive. Fortunately you have all the subtlety and guile you need to reawaken interest. You can do a real service by offering encouragement.

WEDNESDAY, 15TH SEPTEMBER
Mars conjunct Pluto

Ruthlessness is the order of the day as Mars and Pluto move into close conjunction. There is no place for illusions at the moment so you must be prepared to ditch anything that's holding you back. Old guilt and resentments have to go if you are to have a healthy psychological outlook in the future. If another person's faults are damaging your confidence or peace of mind, you'll question the nature of your relationship.

THURSDAY, 16TH SEPTEMBER
Mercury into Libra

There's a certain flexibility entering your career structure as indicated by the presence of Mercury in your Solar area of ambition. You can now turn your acute mind to all sorts of career problems and solve them to everyone's satisfaction, and your own personal advantage. Your powers of persuasion will be heightened, ensuring that you charm bosses and employers to get your own way. Those seeking work should attend interviews because your personality will shine.

FRIDAY, 17TH SEPTEMBER
Mercury trine Neptune

You have arrived at a point where you consider your options, re-examine your aims and ambitions, and question your whole career structure. This may be a painful period since you now realize that a lot of your goals no longer hold any attraction. However, this ruthless appraisal of where you stand is necessary for the development of new ambitions. Any word of advice would be welcome, though you will get through this and come out a stronger, more decisive person.

CAPRICORN

SATURDAY, 18TH SEPTEMBER
Moon square Mercury

There are times when discretion is the better part of valour. Though you may know something that others don't, in professional affairs especially, keep your opinions and knowledge to yourself. Indiscretion now will cost you dear, so if in doubt concerning the reliability of anyone, keep silent.

SUNDAY, 19TH SEPTEMBER
Moon trine Saturn

Common sense rules the day as the Moon makes a positive contact with Saturn. Not for you airy-fairy flights of fancy. Your feet are planted firmly on the ground and won't have much time for sentiment.

MONDAY, 20TH SEPTEMBER
Moon trine Sun

Though you may feel that your dose of luck today is too good to be true, as the day goes on you'll learn to trust the good fortune that comes your way. Your aims and ideals look far more likely to be fulfilled than they have for a long time. Your partner is in tune with your desires, and friends show their support and goodwill. What could be better to start you off on an optimistic phase of achievement?

TUESDAY, 21ST SEPTEMBER
Mercury sextile Pluto

You may be filled with great money-making ideas today but you will need to look a little more deeply at these before acting upon them. There may be something going on behind the scenes in your place of work that will act in your favour when it all comes out into the open.

WEDNESDAY, 22ND SEPTEMBER
Moon opposite Venus

Watch your spending today. It is all too easy to go crazy at this time of the year, but do try to take things easy and to give your credit cards a chance to recover from the last spending spree before starting on the next one! If a friend offers to come shopping with you, leave all your cards, cheque books and money behind, in case you get talked into spending too much.

THURSDAY, 23RD SEPTEMBER
Sun into Libra

The Sun moves decisively into your horoscope area of ambition from today bringing in a month when your worldly progress will achieve absolute priority.

CAPRICORN

You need to feel that what you are doing is worthwhile and has more meaning than simply paying the bills. You may feel the urge to change you career, to make a long-term commitment to a worthwhile cause, or simply to demand recognition for past efforts. However this ambitious phase manifests itself, you can be sure that your prospects are considerably boosted from now on.

FRIDAY, 24TH SEPTEMBER
Mars sextile Uranus

Though common sense dictates a calm, sensible attitude to finances, a sudden hunch will propel you into instant action. A fast profit is likely for many. Mars and Uranus give all the confidence that you could possibly need to pull off the perfect deal!

SATURDAY, 25TH SEPTEMBER
Full Moon

The Full Moon today focuses firmly on family and domestic issues. Perhaps it is time for some straight talking because this is the best opportunity you will get to put an end to home-based or emotional problems. In some ways, it is time to put your cards on the table, yet equally to give credit and take some share of blame in family affairs. Apart from such personal concerns it is time to speak to someone in authority about your ambitions.

SUNDAY, 26TH SEPTEMBER
Moon opposite Mercury

You may not be able to think straight today and you could get yourself into something of a muddle either at home or at work. The trick to surviving this kind of planetary aspect is to keep to the most mundane and routine of tasks and to take plenty of breaks. Don't bother with anything that requires acuity or clarity of mind until the stars have moved on a bit.

MONDAY, 27TH SEPTEMBER
Moon square Neptune

You need some relaxation today without the normal demands made on you by friends and those who are more than friends. Take your mind off material concerns because you're in no state to make far-reaching decisions. In fact, you're in no state to make any sort of decision because your mind is a little foggy just now.

TUESDAY, 28TH SEPTEMBER
Moon conjunct Saturn

The path of true love never runs smoothly, you should know that by now! It is obvious that when the Moon gets chilled by grim Saturn, emotional affairs aren't going to go well at all. Circumstances get in the way of romance. It is said that 'faint heart never won fair lady' (or gentleman), so don't give up yet! If love's worth having, then it's worth fighting for! Be brave!

WEDNESDAY, 29TH SEPTEMBER
Moon trine Neptune

You may feel off-colour or simply in a bad mood. The truth is that there is nothing really wrong with you and there is nothing going on to make you unhappy but that doesn't stop you feeling rather fed up and downhearted. We can all have an off day, even when there is no real reason for it.

THURSDAY, 30TH SEPTEMBER
Moon trine Uranus

When you look at your weekly expenses you could be in for something of a nasty shock as you realize how close to the red you actually are. However, this gloomy view won't last since there is some news on the way which will brighten your outlook considerably. You will see your situation in a new and more optimistic light.

October at a Glance

LOVE	♥	♥	♥	♥	
WORK	★	★	★	★	★
MONEY	£	£	£	£	
HEALTH	✪	✪			
LUCK	♘	♘	♘		

FRIDAY, 1ST OCTOBER
Sun sextile Pluto

Something that has been going on in the background of your life is beginning to come to the fore. This would be a good time to turn a hobby into a money-making venture or to look inside yourself in order to discover talents that you rarely put to good use.

CAPRICORN

SATURDAY, 2ND OCTOBER
Mercury sextile Venus

Since you're obviously in a go-ahead mood it would be far too easy to impulsively race ahead without a thought for anyone else. Yet there is something to be said for making time to chat with a valued friend or colleague. Subtlety is the key to advancement today since a small hint could open up a whole new panorama of experience. Use some charm and you're likely to learn something to your advantage.

SUNDAY, 3RD OCTOBER
Moon square Mercury

If you want any peace now, you'd better keep your mouth firmly shut because you'll get very little sympathy or understanding. The trouble is that you are pretty logical while those around you are too emotional to see anything rationally at all!

MONDAY, 4TH OCTOBER
Moon sextile Sun

You may be faced with a bit of a battle today, but your confidence is high and you seem to have an inner conviction that you can win. To be honest, we think that you are quite right!

TUESDAY, 5TH OCTOBER
Mercury into Scorpio

The swift-moving planet Mercury enters your eleventh Solar house today and gives a remarkable uplift to your social prospects. During the next few weeks you'll find yourself at the centre point of friendly interactions. People will seek you out for the pleasure of your company. It is also a good time to get in contact with distant friends and those you haven't seen for a while. The only fly in the ointment is that you shouldn't expect a small phone bill.

WEDNESDAY, 6TH OCTOBER
Sun trine Uranus

The Sun's positive aspect to Uranus will open your eyes to the boundless potentials of your career prospects. A whole new avenue of endeavour could unexpectedly come to light, and since this aspect also affects a strongly financial area of your chart, it promises to increase your income. Benefits are likely to come as the result of modern innovations and technology. A thorough understanding of computing would be advantageous, so make the effort to keep up to date.

CAPRICORN

THURSDAY, 7TH OCTOBER
Venus into Virgo

Venus enters your Solar ninth house of exploration this month and this may make you slightly restless. Venus is concerned with the pleasures of life and also with leisure activities of all kinds, so explore such ideas as sporting interests, listening to interesting music or going to art galleries. You may want to travel somewhere new and different soon.

FRIDAY, 8TH OCTOBER
Moon trine Neptune

You have a feeling that with the right amount of persuasion, coupled with the necessary investment, you could make a professional killing in the future. Indeed you could, so follow your hunch and give it your best shot!

SATURDAY, 9TH OCTOBER
New Moon

The New Moon today shows the great heights that you could possibly attain. The message is that there's nothing to fear except fear itself. Reach for the stars and you've got it made. Your career should begin to blossom now and you can achieve the kind of respect and status that you are looking for over the next month or so.

SUNDAY, 10TH OCTOBER
Venus trine Jupiter

There's an adventurous outlook to your horoscope today. Venus and Jupiter join forces to open up a chance of travel, or at least to have contact with cultures different from your own. These two lucky planets give you the urge to broaden your experience in some way.

MONDAY, 11TH OCTOBER
Jupiter square Neptune

Money problems loom large today as all opportunities suddenly evaporate and you are left high and dry! Debts and loans are the main area of concern, even so, you will still have the urge to ignore the problem in the hope it will go away. It won't!

TUESDAY, 12TH OCTOBER
Void Moon

This is not a great day on which to decide anything or to start anything new. A void Moon suggests that there are no major planetary aspects being made, either

CAPRICORN

between planets or involving the Sun or the Moon. This is a fairly unusual situation but it does happen from time to time and the only way to deal with it is to stick to your usual routines and do nothing special for a while.

WEDNESDAY, 13TH OCTOBER
Mercury square Uranus

You could be pretty weak-willed today especially if a friend suggests an expensive outing. Not only will you agree immediately, but will be inclined to foot the bill as well, no matter how badly your cash flow is doing. Try to be more sensible with money!

THURSDAY, 14TH OCTOBER
Neptune direct

If your money has been slipping through your fingers recently, a lot of the blame can be aimed at Neptune which has been confusing the financial realities of your life for some time. From today though, the watery planet resumes direct motion, clearing up some major worries as it does so. At last you'll be able to work out the precise state of your finances.

FRIDAY, 15TH OCTOBER
Moon conjunct Mars

You're keeping a lot of unexpressed frustration under control early on in the day but internal pressure is building. It is no answer to keep negative feelings bottled up, but exploding in all directions isn't a good idea either. Direct your anger at the root cause of the problem, not take it out on all around you. You'll be tempted to plot an intricate and devastating revenge, but you should try to prove your detractors wrong by doing the best you can.

SATURDAY, 16TH OCTOBER
Mercury opposite Saturn

Children or younger family members may see you are being the silly, irresponsible and childish one, while they are sober-sided, serious and very adult. Perhaps they are right! You do seem to be in a particularly soppy frame of mind right now.

SUNDAY, 17TH OCTOBER
Mars into Capricorn

Mars enters your own sign of the zodiac today and it will spend a few weeks there, bringing zest, energy and a welcome element of fun into your life. You seem to be on a 'roll' at the moment, and as long as you keep up the momentum, there is no reason why you should not be able to reach your objectives.

CAPRICORN

MONDAY, 18TH OCTOBER
Venus square Pluto

You could become totally obsessed with a new idea today and will be determined to convert everyone around you before you've thought it through yourself. Slow down, and take some time to ponder.

TUESDAY, 19TH OCTOBER
Moon square Saturn

An absence of ready cash could put you in a gloomy frame of mind today, but you should realize by now that this problem is purely temporary, and like everything else, will soon pass.

WEDNESDAY, 20TH OCTOBER
Moon sextile Jupiter

'Out of the mouths of babes', well perhaps not exactly babes, yet younger people will provide a stimulation and enthusiasm that will reawaken a positive mental attitude. Just as long as you remember that you are never too old to learn, there's a valuable lesson in store from a childlike teacher. Perhaps you too can learn to see the world with a sense of wonder.

THURSDAY, 21ST OCTOBER
Moon opposite Venus

You seem to be giving up the thought of becoming a hard-headed business person today and becoming a dreamy, sensitive and kindly soul instead. Your soft centre is showing through your usual crusty exterior and your response to others will be tender and affectionate. This is a marvellous day on which to whisper sweet nothings to your lover and to steer clear of any serious negotiating.

FRIDAY, 22ND OCTOBER
Sun square Neptune

Caution should be your watchword today. If you trust anyone with something valuable, a treasured possession, cash or even a confidence, you'll end up regretting it. It doesn't matter how well you know the person concerned because even the best of us can make mistakes, and your friend is no exception. Do not exclude the possibility that mischief was intended on purpose. Take care!

SATURDAY, 23RD OCTOBER
Sun into Scorpio

As the Sun makes its yearly entrance into your eleventh Solar house, you can be sure that friends and acquaintances are going to have a powerful influence on your

CAPRICORN

prospects. The Sun's harmonious angle to your own sign gives an optimism and vitality to your outgoing nature. Social life will increase in importance over the next month. You'll be a popular and much sought-after person. Obstacles that have irritated you will now be swept away.

SUNDAY, 24TH OCTOBER
Full Moon

Your creative soul and romantic yearnings come under the influence of today's Full Moon, so it is time to take stock of those things in your life that no longer give any emotional satisfaction. Children and younger people may need a word or two of advice and the love lives of all around you will become the centre of interest. Your own romantic prospects may see an upturn too.

MONDAY, 25TH OCTOBER
Venus trine Saturn

There is a touch of heartache about today's stars even though Saturn and Venus are in good aspect to each other. It may be that even though there's nothing seriously wrong in a romance, you may be unavoidably separated from a loved one for a while.

TUESDAY, 26TH OCTOBER
Moon opposite Mercury

Your mind may be set on having fun with your friends but try not to overload your already stretched schedule. Practical affairs have to be dealt with whether you're in the mood or not. You want to party but you'll only end up over-tired and edgy. It may be a case of all work and no play, but it is better in the long run. Resist friends who insist that you be sociable. It is only replacing one duty with another.

WEDNESDAY, 27TH OCTOBER
Moon opposite Pluto

Any genuine need will become a cause to be taken up and pursued with vigour. You are in a crusading mood, inspired by the mixed rays of the Moon and Pluto. In fact, you will be prepared to go to great lengths to help those less fortunate than you. In all this compassion, spare a thought for yourself. It wouldn't do to wear yourself out while alleviating the suffering of others.

THURSDAY, 28TH OCTOBER
Mercury sextile Neptune

Though you often like to appear hard, it would be difficult not to show how kind

CAPRICORN

and charitable you actually are today. You simply can't ignore a plea for help, whether it is via the media and concerns a worthy cause or from a friend in need. Your generosity is invaluable. Your philosophy embraces the concept of selfless consideration of others.

FRIDAY, 29TH OCTOBER
Moon opposite Mars

If your other half has got any idea of chaining you to the kitchen sink, then someone is in for a surprise. You're in no mood to pander to the desires of anyone other than yourself, so any attempt to make you toe the line will result in a furious outburst. You are a positive dynamo of energy today and should seek some more constructive way of burning off the excess. Otherwise your close relationships could resemble a medium-sized war by this evening.

SATURDAY, 30TH OCTOBER
Mercury into Sagittarius

You will find yourself in a more introspective mood for a few weeks because Mercury, planet of the mind, enters the most secret and inward-looking portion of your horoscope from today. This is the start of a period when you'll want to understand the inner being, your own desires and motivations. Too much hectic life will prove a distraction now so go by instinct and seek out solitude when you feel like it.

SUNDAY, 31ST OCTOBER
Moon square Sun

You have expended so much energy recently that it is about time you cut down on all your furious activities and took it easy for a while. Your passions are very strong at the moment with all these sudden attractions racing into your life, but it is important that you take some time to think and to simply sit down and rest. If you don't at least try some relaxation, you'll be back to a stressed-out state in no time.

CAPRICORN

November at a Glance

LOVE	♥				
WORK	★	★	★	★	★
MONEY	£	£	£		
HEALTH	✪	✪	✪		
LUCK	♘				

MONDAY, 1ST NOVEMBER
Void Moon

Today is one of those odd days when there are no important planetary aspects being made, not even to the Moon. The best way to tackle this kind of day is to stick to your usual routine and to avoid starting anything new or tackling anything of major importance. If you do decide to do something large today, then it will take longer and be harder to cope with than it would normally.

TUESDAY, 2ND NOVEMBER
Moon square Mercury

You could be having some kind of crisis of conscience today because you are finding it hard to go along with the beliefs or the behaviour of others. If others insist on breaking the law or on behaving in a particularly spiteful or nasty manner to a third party, then keep yourself right out of the situation and do what you know to be right. Keep to the straight and narrow and you can't go wrong.

WEDNESDAY, 3RD NOVEMBER
Moon trine Saturn

Parental figures and those in positions of authority over you will prove to be very helpful today. If you are experiencing difficulties in a creative project, ask an expert for advice.

THURSDAY, 4TH NOVEMBER
Moon sextile Mercury

Your mind is working much more clearly than it has been lately and you will soon begin to see answers to some of your problems. You may need to negotiate for something at work or you may have to ask for something far more subtle, such

CAPRICORN

as being treated with respect and understanding by others. You need to behave in a totally professional manner rather than projecting a lackadaisical image.

FRIDAY, 5TH NOVEMBER
Moon trine Uranus

Unexpected good news is seeking you out today. Both financially and in the professional sphere there are developments that are going to do you a lot of good. You won't quite know how to react, yet instinctively you will know that this is the opportunity you've been looking for. Go on with confidence.

SATURDAY, 6TH NOVEMBER
Sun opposite Saturn

Any criticism of your actions, your work or your appearance, will hit hard today. You are feeling very sensitive and will be prone to self-doubt and despondency, so any harsh comment will send your self-esteem spiralling down. Try to remember that it is only an opinion, so do something you enjoy to bolster your flagging ego.

SUNDAY, 7TH NOVEMBER
Sun sextile Mars

The emphasis today will be on your social life rather than home affairs or your work. Friends may take you off to some kind of local entertainment or you may be invited to an unexpectedly good party. This is a wonderful day for romance, especially for females. Men may enjoy sporting activities in the company of friends.

MONDAY, 8TH NOVEMBER
New Moon

There is no doubt that issues surrounding friendship and trust are very important. The New Moon in your horoscopic area of social activities ensures that encounters with interesting people will yield new and enduring friendships. Though your mood has tended to vary between optimism and despair recently, the New Moon cannot fail to increase your confidence and vitality.

TUESDAY, 9TH NOVEMBER
Mercury into Scorpio

This is the time to join others and to become part of a team. So if you play any games or if you enjoy any kind of group actitivy, get your pals together and have fun. Friends and acquaintances will take you out of yourself and you will enjoy their company to the full.

CAPRICORN

WEDNESDAY, 10TH NOVEMBER
Moon sextile Uranus

Money luck is in the stars as the Moon and Uranus will either bring cash your way or show you the means of making some. However, it may not be wise to reveal that you have received this good fortune.

THURSDAY, 11TH NOVEMBER
Moon trine Jupiter

There will be a couple of lucky breaks that help you to sort out a number of sticky family or relationship problems that have been bugging you. Help will come from hidden or unexpected sources and you will be on the receiving end of more kindness than you can usually expect to find from the world around you. Older female relatives will come to your aid, either by helping out in a practical way, or by smoothing over ruffled family feathers for you.

FRIDAY, 12TH NOVEMBER
Moon square Venus

You would love some quiet relaxation today but some well-meaning friends will be determined to drag you kicking and screaming from your shell. It won't matter that you would like some solitude, or even some intimate time alone with a special person, your friends have decided that the social scene is where you belong. You will have to be firm about this, because subtle hints won't work.

SATURDAY, 13TH NOVEMBER
Moon conjunct Mars

A determined and businesslike attitude prevails today. Your ability to follow through on an original impulse will certainly win respect, even if you do meet a little opposition along the way. Opposition won't bother you now though. In fact, you'll relish the challenge. You can accomplish wonders. Just one word of warning: your fiery impatience is strongly stimulated today too, so take care when driving or generally rushing about.

SUNDAY, 14TH NOVEMBER
Saturn square Uranus

Romantic dreams are frustrated today by Saturn, while Uranus causes a leak in your cash reservoir. It seems that you can't win at the moment, so don't try! Avoid confrontations and wait for a better day!

CAPRICORN

MONDAY, 15TH NOVEMBER
Moon square Saturn

Financial good fortune shouldn't go to your head, neither should you spend too much to please others today. Let caution be your watchword otherwise you'll be back in a perilous financial state before you know it.

TUESDAY, 16TH NOVEMBER
Mercury sextile Mars

This is a great day for having fun and for temporarily shelving all those boring and trying responsibilities. You may feel in a kind of 'breakout' mood in which you leave your normal routine behind and spend the day doing things that are new and unusual. Your mind will be buzzing with new ideas and you may profitably spend a good part of the day discussing these with colleagues or friends.

WEDNESDAY, 17TH NOVEMBER
Venus sextile Pluto

You are not usually a cold, hard schemer, but today you might just be. You've got an eye for the main chance and have the power to manipulate others into giving you exactly what you want. Realizing that the direct approach isn't always the right one, your strategies are prepared in advance. That's all well and good as long as you aren't taking unfair advantage.

THURSDAY, 18TH NOVEMBER
Moon trine Mercury

You won't be able to complain of being kept in the dark today because there seem to be messages, letters, phone calls and faxes coming at you from all directions. You may need to attend to paperwork or to details of some kind at your place of work. Try to keep all these bits of paper together in one place (especially those that relate to money), because they may get lost.

FRIDAY, 19TH NOVEMBER
Moon sextile Neptune

An old memory resurfaces today. Perhaps, the rediscovery of a faded photograph will send you on a trip down Memory Lane. At least the memories will be happy ones and should bring a smile to your face.

SATURDAY, 20TH NOVEMBER
Venus trine Uranus

It is a day for a windfall! The stunning combination of Venus and Uranus could well bring you a gift of extra cash. If you are truly in luck, this could mean a new and unexpected source of income. If not that, then a competition prize could be on its way. Professionally speaking, this is the time for some unconventional thinking. Old, worn-out methods won't do if you're trying to win the approval of people in power.

SUNDAY, 21ST NOVEMBER
Mars square Jupiter

There may be differences of opinion in connection with the vexed subject of money. If you are not directly in the firing line, then leave your friends, relatives or colleagues to work out for themselves who should be spending what. If you are dragged into the argument or if you are also accused of overspending, try to avoid getting too angry. It seems that all this activity stems from a power struggle that is going on around you.

MONDAY, 22ND NOVEMBER
Sun into Sagittarius

The Sun moves into your house of secrets and psychology today making you attuned to your own inner world of dreams and imagination. For the next month you'll be very aware of the hurdles that face you, and all those things that tend to restrict your freedom. However, your imagination and almost psychic insight will provide the necessary clues to overcome these obstacles. Issues of privacy are very important for the next few weeks.

TUESDAY, 23RD NOVEMBER
Full Moon

Something is coming to a head in relation to your job. This is not a major crisis and there is absolutely no need to flounce out of a perfectly good position, but there is a problem that should be solved before you can continue on in a happy and peaceful frame of mind. You may have to sort out what your role is and which part of the job other people should be doing, because it looks as if you are carrying too much of the load at the moment.

WEDNESDAY, 24TH NOVEMBER
Moon trine Venus

Your job, career or business is taking precedence just at the moment. This is probably not the time to be terribly creative or experimental in what you are doing but simply to plod along your usual path and do what you have to do. You may have nothing more exciting than household chores to occupy yourself with now but these have to be done and you might as well do them properly.

CAPRICORN

THURSDAY, 25TH NOVEMBER
Sun sextile Neptune

Though you are generally a trusting soul, you've been burned once too often to take anything at face value now. Anyone who tries to con you today is in for a nasty shock since you've got the penetrating insight to see though the mask to the true motive underneath. In financial affairs, your shrewdness ensures monetary gain.

FRIDAY, 26TH NOVEMBER
Mars into Aquarius

Mars moves into your Solar house of finance and income from today and draws your attention to urgent matters that should have been dealt with long ago. If you have let your economic realities slide, then now is the time to rectify the situation before the expense becomes unbearable. You can focus an abundance of energy towards increasing your income. Unnecessary expenditures will be reviewed and some much needed economies made. Swift action is your forte.

SATURDAY, 27TH NOVEMBER
Moon opposite Neptune

You and your partner will both be in an extremely amorous frame of mind today. This would be great if you didn't have to go to work, cope with chores or put up with constant interruptions from the family!

SUNDAY, 28TH NOVEMBER
Moon square Mercury

It is a very confusing day on most fronts when your mental processes are slowed down and clouded by the Moon's influence. Red tape, documents and official correspondence will leave you paralysed with indecision. All you want to do is escape and possibly ask a friend to help out, unfortunately that won't do much good, since friends are as confused as you are. This is not a good day to deal with far-reaching business or financial affairs anyway so try to put them off.

MONDAY, 29TH NOVEMBER
Mars conjunct Neptune

Your heart is telling you to spend, spend! Worse still, your head is in no mood to stop you. Hopefully, you will resist too much of this temptation before you run out of money altogether.

CAPRICORN

TUESDAY, 30TH NOVEMBER
Moon trine Saturn

Though temptation abounds, you have the will-power, self-control and enough personal esteem to resist it today. Holding yourself to the tried and true will be best for you in the long run, and you already know that better than anyone else.

December at a Glance

LOVE	♥	♥		
WORK	★	★	★	★
MONEY	£			
HEALTH	✛	✛		
LUCK	♘	♘	♘	

WEDNESDAY, 1ST DECEMBER
Venus opposite Jupiter

This is a poor day on which to take chances. If you have to leave your house for any length of time, make sure that you lock up properly and set the burglar alarm (if you have one). Take care when travelling and guard against doing silly things at work.

THURSDAY, 2ND DECEMBER
Moon sextile Sun

If a want a job done properly, you'll have to do it yourself today. This is no great hardship since you will actually enjoy what you are doing as long as you are left in peace to get on with it.

FRIDAY, 3RD DECEMBER
Moon opposite Jupiter

If you are looking for a job today, you could be disappointed. Don't take this too seriously. It may be that the people you have applied to could use you, but at a later date, or it may be that this was simply the wrong kind of job for you to apply for. The same goes for your chances of promotion or for a raise because this is simply not the day to bother to ask for either.

CAPRICORN

SATURDAY, 4TH DECEMBER
Moon square Neptune

Hope overrules experience today and you could head off into cloud-cuckoo-land if you don't keep at least one foot on the ground. Optimism is a good thing, but even that can be taken too far!

SUNDAY, 5TH DECEMBER
Venus into Scorpio

Venus moves into your eleventh house of friendship and group activities today, bringing a few weeks of happiness and harmony for you and your friends. You could fall in love under this transit or you could reaffirm your feelings towards a current partner. You should be looking and feeling rather good but, if not, this is the time to spend some money on your appearance and to do something about any nagging health problems.

MONDAY, 6TH DECEMBER
Sun sextile Uranus

Any Solar contact with Uranus is bound to bring a few surprises in its wake. Today is no exception so follow your instincts where money is concerned, even if they lead you away from the straight and narrow. You'll profit in the end as long as you aren't sidetracked by the more conventional views of friends and colleagues. You know best at the moment, and it is up to you what you do with your cash.

TUESDAY, 7TH DECEMBER
New Moon

The world of romance is especially attractive on a day when your dreams and fantasies take over your life. The New Moon points the way to new emotional experiences in the future, but you mustn't cling to the past because of misplaced loyalty or guilt. Some people are leaving your life, but if you were honest, you'd admit that they're no real loss. Follow your instincts and your dreams may well come true.

WEDNESDAY, 8TH DECEMBER
Venus square Neptune

Don't accept anything on face value today. There are some unscrupulous people around you now and they'd quite like to part you from some of your cash. Let caution be your watchword. Don't fall for any sob stories or be too ready to bail out a supposed friend. Any charitable appeals should be checked out to make sure that they are what they seem. Sentiment, no matter how laudable, shouldn't be allowed to overrule your common sense.

CAPRICORN

THURSDAY, 9TH DECEMBER
Moon sextile Venus

There is the prospect of new faces in your life today. If you're invited to any social gathering, you'd better make up your mind to go, because you'll certainly miss out if you don't attend. If, by some chance, no invitations are forthcoming, then invite your friends to a local bar or club. Good company is vital to you now. You need to feel part of a close-knit group for your personality to shine.

FRIDAY, 10TH DECEMBER
Mars square Saturn

Children and young people may cause you extra expense today. They may need equipment for sports or some other kind of hobby. Or you may choose to spend money on a hobby or a leisure pursuit, only to find that this was a waste of time.

SATURDAY, 11TH DECEMBER
Mercury into Sagittarius

You may receive a surprise letter or phone call from someone whom you had relegated to the background of your life. Another possibility is that you will have to spend the next couple of weeks sorting out some kind of outstanding paperwork or even a muddle which is related to your work. Now is the time to put right any misunderstandings and apologize to someone if this is appropriate.

SUNDAY, 12TH DECEMBER
Mercury sextile Neptune

Though you will be inclined to play your cards close to your chest, it might be an idea to have a confidential chat to a financial expert about some matter which has been troubling you. The problem will be easier to sort out than you think!

MONDAY, 13TH DECEMBER
Moon sextile Sun

A mystery will be resolved today and something that you thought you had lost will suddenly turn up. If you have misunderstood someone else's motives, you will now be able to see what has really been behind their strange behaviour.

TUESDAY, 14TH DECEMBER
Mars conjunct Uranus

The finances are going through some fast and furious changes today, and the conjunction of Mars and Uranus shows that this influence is set to continue for a while. You could overspend on a bargain at the moment, and yet receive a windfall that will balance the budget once more.

CAPRICORN

WEDNESDAY, 15TH DECEMBER
Venus opposite Saturn

The path of true love is not going to run smoothly today. Someone close may be surly and awkward but you mustn't feel too guilty since you are not the cause. There will be no point in causing a confrontation or offering tea and sympathy. Just leave your lover to it and he or she will come around in their own time.

THURSDAY, 16TH DECEMBER
Moon sextile Neptune

Money and Neptune don't really mix, so take care you are not taken in by plausible people or shoddy goods today. The good news is that the positive aspect to the Moon will tend to steer you away from trouble.

FRIDAY, 17TH DECEMBER
Sun trine Jupiter

Get set to take off to foreign climes. You seem keen to escape from it all and explore a different part of the world. You may have a secret desire to visit a particular place and, if so, why not do something about it today?

SATURDAY, 18TH DECEMBER
Mercury conjunct Pluto

There is so much going on behind the scenes in your life that is impossible to keep track of it all. You seem destined to make some kind of important transformation in your life soon and you are in the planning stages of this now.

SUNDAY, 19TH DECEMBER
Moon conjunct Saturn

You will be rather listless and prone to depression today. Perhaps a love affair isn't going too well at the moment, or a young person is giving you cause for worry. Don't get too stressed, this influence will soon pass.

MONDAY, 20TH DECEMBER
Jupiter into Aries

You will have no trouble in picking up the undercurrents of another person's feelings, since Jupiter, the planet of broad understanding, enters your Solar house of hearth and home from today. Financial stability is a feature of the giant planet's presence in this house, so paying the bills shouldn't present a problem for a while.

CAPRICORN

TUESDAY, 21ST DECEMBER
Moon opposite Pluto

Stubbornness is not going to get you anywhere today. You can't just close your eyes to obvious facts and wish them away. Adaptation is the key to success so whether your troubles involve a work or health matter, sort it out at once. You may not solve this irritation but at least you will know where you stand and that is some comfort.

WEDNESDAY, 22ND DECEMBER
Sun into Capricorn

The Sun moves into your own sign today bringing with it a lifting of your spirits and a gaining of confidence all round. Your birthday will soon be here and we hope that it will be a good one for you. You may see more of your family than is usual now and there should be some socializing and partying to look forward to. Music belongs to the realm of the Sun, so spoil yourself with a musical treat soon.

THURSDAY, 23RD DECEMBER
Full Moon

Your close relationships come into focus under the influence of the Full Moon. One-to-one affairs need extra understanding and tolerance so be prepared to talk over any differences that have developed. You will probably find that problems are the result of misunderstandings rather than any real falling out. Take this opportunity to sort out your emotional commitments before more serious damage is done.

FRIDAY, 24TH DECEMBER
Venus square Mars

There is rather a tense atmosphere about you on Christmas Eve as the energies of Mars and Venus spread disharmony amongst your friends and associates. You don't want to be involved in other people's marital crises, or to take sides in a dispute between friends, but the only way you will avoid it is by making yourself scarce for a while. If you don't want a dispute of your own, then don't borrow or lend money.

SATURDAY, 25TH DECEMBER
Moon trine Pluto

You will be in no mood to tolerate vague promises or needless mysteries on Christmas Day. If someone around you is being evasive you will be determined to find out exactly what's going on. OK, so it may not be your business but that's

CAPRICORN

not going to stop you once you've got the scent. You can be a regular sleuth when you want to be. Have a Merry Christmas!

SUNDAY, 26TH DECEMBER
Mercury sextile Mars

Your mind is going at full pelt and it will be extremely easy for you to find the answers to a number of problems just by thinking about them for a while. Whether what you are trying to sort out is practical, financial, emotional or spiritual, you seem almost to be guided by some higher power today.

MONDAY, 27TH DECEMBER
Mercury trine Jupiter

It might be best if you kept your own counsel for a while. After all, you need to be certain about a few things before you commit yourself. Mercury and Jupiter promise that all will be well, but you will still want to wait and see.

TUESDAY, 28TH DECEMBER
Moon square Mercury

Though your thoughts are profound and have deep significance to the lives of those around you, you can't seem to find the right words to express them. If you persevere you will only end up confusing everyone, including yourself, so it would be better to be silent for a while to let the ideas gel a little more.

WEDNESDAY, 29TH DECEMBER
Moon square Sun

You have to work and to get on, even when you don't feel like it, and today you don't feel like it one little bit! If you are a bit off-colour or just not in the mood to make the effort, do what you have to do and leave the rest of the chores until you feel in the mood to tackle them.

THURSDAY, 30TH DECEMBER
Mars sextile Jupiter

You are keen to expand your horizons, so take a look around and see how you can make your life just that little bit bigger and better than it is at present. You can take a bit of a financial gamble today if you want because the planets suggest that your luck is holding up quite well.

FRIDAY, 31ST DECEMBER
Venus into Sagittarius

As Venus enters your Solar house of secrets and psychology, it is obvious that the

CAPRICORN

next year will increase the importance of discretion in your romantic life. You will find that it will be wise to draw a veil over the more intimate side of your nature, and you'll be less inclined to confide your deepest secrets even to your closest friends. Quiet interludes with the one you love will be far more attractive than painting the town red just now. Happy New Century!